# Third Sector Organisations, Asylum Seekers and Refugees

Matthew Davis

# Third Sector Organisations, Asylum Seekers and Refugees

## Support During Covid-19 and Post-Pandemic

Matthew Davis
Law School
University of Wolverhampton
Wolverhampton, UK

ISBN 978-3-031-85136-0      ISBN 978-3-031-85137-7   (eBook)
https://doi.org/10.1007/978-3-031-85137-7

This Palgrave Macmillan imprint is published by the registered company Springer Nature
Switzerland AG
The registered company address is: Gewerbestrasse 11, 6330 Cham, Switzerland

*Competing Interests* The author has no competing interests to declare that are relevant to the content of this manuscript.

# CONTENTS

# Contents

# ABOUT THE AUTHOR

**Dr Matthew Davis** is a Lecturer in Immigration Law and Researcher in International Migration. Matthew holds a PhD in International Law, Human Rights and Criminal Justice from the University of Birmingham. He teaches Nationality, International Migration and Asylum Law and is a Fellow of the Academics Stand Against Poverty Global Justice Program at Yale University.

Dr Matthew Davis conducts research on modern slavery and human trafficking from both a crime control perspective and adopts a victim centred approach to assisting and supporting victims of human trafficking and exploitation. He has previous experience of working in a safehouse for victims of human trafficking. His work lends himself to suggesting solutions to complex issues of identification and detection of more victims in the UK.

# CHAPTER 1

# Introduction and Context

**Abstract** The phenomenon of human smugglers exploiting vulnerable migrants by offering safe passage to the UK via the Channel represents a serious threat to UK security. There is an ongoing and significant problem with human smugglers facilitating small boats to carry migrants across the English Channel to the UK. Many tragedies have been reported at sea where people are drowning from overcrowded dinghies and inflatable boats which capsize whilst trying to cross the English Channel. The present response from the UK government in combatting this crime takes the view that the migrants themselves are to blame for this, rather than tackling the organised crime groups facilitating these operations. Finally, the chapter briefly references the now in limbo proposed Rwanda plan which seeks to remove migrants from the UK to Rwanda to have their claims for asylum assessed outside of the UK signifies a significant move to deterring vulnerable asylum seekers and refugees away from the UK's international legal obligations which have been in force and adopted for many decades.

**Keywords** Asylum seekers · Refugees · Small Boats · Organised criminal groups · Human Smuggling

© The Author(s), under exclusive license to Springer Nature Switzerland AG 2025
M. Davis, *Third Sector Organisations, Asylum Seekers and Refugees*,
https://doi.org/10.1007/978-3-031-85137-7_1

At the time of this research being carried out, the 2-year anniversary of the deadliest loss of life in the English Channel for more than 40 years occurred when 27 people (mostly from Iran or Iraq including a pregnant woman and three children) drowned trying to cross the Channel in an inflatable boat on 24 November 2021.[1]

Asylum seekers and refugees crossing the English Channel in small boats has been a phenomenon since 2018. Prior to Brexit, many asylum seekers would seek to reach the UK via lorries but since the implementation of more stringent checks and surveillance measures at the border has made this route riskier for people to get caught by Border Immigration Officers. Human smugglers have instead used the English Channel to facilitate border crossings with many asylum seekers paying organised crime groups to provide them with small boats to travel across the water to the UK.

The numbers of people involved in this phenomenon have steadily increased. During 2018 there were 299 people came to the UK in small boats. In 2019 there were 1,843 people, in 2020 there were 8,466, and in 2021 there were 28,526. In 2022, this figure substantially jumped to 45,755.[2] In 2023, the numbers dropped to 29,437,[3] and as of 31 March 2024, 4,993 people had crossed the English Channel.[4] On 14 Nov 2024, it was stated that 32,900 migrants had entered the UK via a small boat.[5]

---

[1] Marine Accident Investigation Branch (MAIB) Accident Report, "Report on the investigation into the flooding and partial sinking of an inflatable migrant boat resulting in the loss of at least 27 lives in the Dover Strait on 24 November 2021," Report No 7/2023 November 2023.

[2] Figures from the Migration Observatory, "People crossing the English Channel in small boats," 21 July 2023, accessed at https://migrationobservatory.ox.ac.uk/resources/briefings/people-crossing-the-english-channel-in-small-boats/.

[3] BBC News, "How many people cross the Channel in small boats and how many claim asylum in the UK," accessed at https://www.bbc.co.uk/news/uk-53699511.

[4] Ben Morris, "Record 5,000 cross Channel to UK in first three months of 2024," *The Guardian*, 31 March 2024, accessed at https://www.theguardian.com/uk-news/2024/mar/31/record-number-channel-crossings-small-boats-uk-immigration.

[5] Home Office Data, "Small boat activity in the English Channel," 14 November 2024 accessed at https://www.gov.uk/government/publications/migrants-detected-crossing-the-english-channel-in-small-boats.

Out of the 45,755 people who arrived in the UK via small boats in 2022[6] it was identified that the nationalities comprised of seven countries. These were Albania, Afghanistan, Iran, Iraq, Syria, Eritrea and Sudan.[7] It has been documented that 90% of people who arrived in small boats between 2018 and June 2023 applied for asylum,[8] with 65% of those having their claims accepted by the Home Office.[9]

The UK Government has made numerous attempts to stop migrants coming to the UK to seek asylum. Despite that there is no evidence to support the view that migrants are seeking to use asylum as a way of gaining entry to the UK by 'gaming the system,'[10]; they acknowledge that cooperation with other European States is required to combat the problem. To help combat the problem effectively from either side of the Channel, the UK signed a deal with France which will see a new detention centre established in France with more emphasis from the French to patrol beaches using improved technology.[11] Substantial funding will be spent in the next two years on this issue with around £124 million

---

[6] BBC News, "How many people cross the Channel in small boats and how many claim asylum in the UK," accessed at https://www.bbc.co.uk/news/uk-53699511.

[7] Marley Morris and Amreen Qureshi, "Understanding the rise in channel crossings," Institute for public policy research, October 2022 at 3.

[8] Georgina Sturge, "Asylum Statistics," 1 March 2024 at 32.

[9] Home Office, "Official Statistics Irregular migration to the UK, year ending June 2023," Updated 14 November 2023, accessed at https://www.gov.uk/government/statistics/irregular-migration-to-the-uk-year-ending-june-2023/irregular-migration-to-the-uk-year-ending-june-2023#:~:text=Of%20the%2010%2C377%20Albanian%20small,or%20another%20type%20of%20leave.

[10] Matthew Lodge and Greg Heffer, "Asylum seekers are 'gaming the system' to remain in the UK and '50% of migrants are adults pretending to be children', Suella Braverman claims just days after threatening to leave European Convention on Human Rights," *The Guardian*, 29 September 2023, accessed at https://www.dailymail.co.uk/news/article-12576645/Asylum-seekers-gaming-remain-UK-50-migrants-adults-pretending-children-Suella-Braverman-claims-just-days-threatening-leave-European-Convention-Human-Rights.html.

[11] Prime Minister's Office Press Statement, "Prime Minister agrees unprecedented measures to tackle illegal immigration alongside France," 10 March 2023, accessed at https://www.gov.uk/government/news/prime-minister-agrees-unprecedented-measures-to-tackle-illegal-migration-alongside-france.

committed to 2023/24, £168 million for 2024/25 and £184 million in 2025/26.[12]

The UK Government has also taken legislative steps to criminalise asylum seekers seeking to claim asylum in the UK after arriving via small boats.[13] As a further deterrence, the previous Conservative Government sort to implement the Rwanda policy. As part of this policy the UK signed a Memorandum of Understanding with Rwanda on 14 May 2022 which detailed a plan under which any refugee who came to the UK to seek asylum but was deemed 'inadmissible' by the government could be deported to Rwanda.[14]

The Government has encountered many legal and political issues trying to get this policy implemented. After numerous challenges were heard by courts arguing that Rwanda is not a safe country, and that the policy would violate the human rights of asylum seekers and breaches international law, Supreme Court held on 16 November 2023 that Rwanda is not a safe country, and consequently held that the Rwanda scheme is unlawful.[15] In response to the Supreme Court ruling, the Government took two steps. The first was to draft a UK-Rwanda treaty[16] which sets out the arrangements, roles and responsibilities of parties for processing asylum seekers, and the second was to legislate that Rwanda is a safe country through the Safety of Rwanda (Asylum and Immigration Bill).[17]

---

[12] Melanie Gower, "Irregular Migration: A timeline of UK-French cooperation," Research Briefing Number 9681, House of Commons Library, 22 March 2023 at 3.

[13] See Nationality & Borders Act 2022 and Illegal Migration Act 2023.

[14] See Home Office Policy Paper, "Memorandum of Understanding between the government of the United Kingdom of Great Britain and Northern Ireland and the government of the Republic of Rwanda for the provision of an asylum partnership arrangement," 14 April 2022, accessed at https://www.gov.uk/government/publications/memorandum-of-understanding-mou-between-the-uk-and-rwanda/memorandum-of-understanding-between-the-government-of-the-united-kingdom-of-great-britain-and-northern-ireland-and-the-government-of-the-republic-of-r.

[15] R (on the application of AAA (Syria) and others) (Respondents/Cross Appellants) v Secretary of State for the Home Department (Appellant/Cross Respondent) [2023] UKSC 42.

[16] UK-Rwanda treaty: provision of an asylum partnership Published 5 December 2023—https://www.gov.uk/government/publications/uk-rwanda-treaty-provision-of-an-asylum-partnership/uk-rwanda-treaty-provision-of-an-asylum-partnership-accessible.

[17] Safety of Rwanda (Asylum and Immigration) Bill, 7 March 2024 accessed at https://bills.parliament.uk/publications/54559/documents/4541.

At the time of writing (April 2024), this Bill is going through the House of Lords. The UK government is also seeking to introduce a scheme for failed asylum seekers to voluntarily leave the UK and go to Rwanda in exchange for £3,000.[18]

The following section explains the methodology of the research, the justifications for this research and how the research was conducted out with the cooperation of staff from AX to establish the various types of work the organisation does to protect asylum seekers and refugees given the previous discussion outlining the contextual situation which illustrates a deterrence approach against asylum seekers trying to get to the UK to claim asylum.

---

[18] Kate Whannel, "UK to pay failed asylum seekers to move to Rwanda under new scheme," *BBC News*, 13 March 2024, accessed at https://www.bbc.co.uk/news/uk-pol itics-68550404#:~:text=Failed%20asylum%20seekers%20are%20to,return%20to%20their% 20home%20country.

# CHAPTER 2

# The Approaches Carrying Out Research with Organisation AX

**Abstract** The understanding of the issues, challenges and barriers of frontline staff who work with asylum seekers by understanding how Covid-19 affected their support work is often overlooked and not widely reported. Many organisations work diligently and without much media attention and are motivated by their mission to help and support vulnerable individuals from marginalised social groups. This research adopts a Constructivist Grounded Theory (CGT) which is a qualitative research method that involves co-constructing theories with participants. It is based on the theory that we all form views based on our own life experiences. As this work is multi-disciplinary, this approach is justified and used in many examples of social science research. The views of staff are heard within the research to give meaning to the work that they do and understand how their work impacts the lives of asylum seekers and refugees. It also is used as a means of reflection as to their own emotions, and feeling based on their experiences during the pandemic helping others. Similarly, the views and opinions of asylum seekers are necessary as they describe the impact that the pandemic had on them and the way they were still accommodated by staff during the social restrictions which were in place at that time.

**Keywords** Third Sector Organisations · Covid-19 · Pandemic · Constructivist Grounded Theory

M. Davis, *Third Sector Organisations, Asylum Seekers and Refugees*, https://doi.org/10.1007/978-3-031-85137-7_2

Significant research has been conducted focussing on the lived experience of asylum seekers,[1] and other vulnerable groups within society.[2]

This research takes a different perspective by investigating how a third sector organisation helps and supports asylum seekers and refugees and the ways in which they do this given the potential issues, barriers and challenges many organisations must overcome alongside their work.

Testimonies obtained from discussions of staff from a specific front-line organisation show how they adapted to the pandemic and highlight how lessons can be learnt from helping and supporting migrants during this period. It seeks to pinpoint the needs of staff which should be addressed by employers of third sector organisations to improve efficiency and wellbeing from an operational viewpoint, a mental health lens and psychological perspective. The research effectively examines how frontline organisations need to change given the social, economic and political challenges faced by asylum seekers and refugees in accessing support alongside the impact of new Government immigration and asylum policies alongside new legislation which was brought in during that time.

This research is beneficial for several reasons. It is useful because this type of research is original as it has not been done previously undertaken by any other researcher. The organisation has not engaged with researchers before about their work and therefore this research is novel and offers a different perspective. The content is significant because it explains the challenges of the organisation during the pandemic and the issues asylum seekers and refugees faced and continued to experience after Covid-19. Most of what happened during the pandemic was relatively not heard about given the isolationist way many people and organisations adjusted to live and work during this time due to lack of face-to-face physical contact. Consequently, it is only now that we are learning about what exactly transpired during the years of the pandemic. The work provides a timely examination and reflective practice on what happened during the

---

[1] Helen Liebling, Shani Burke, Simon Goodman and Daniel Zasada, "Understanding the experiences of asylum seekers," (2014) International Journal of Migration, Health, and Social Care, Vol. 10, No. 4, 207 and Thomas Hoare, Andrew Vidgen and Neil P Roberts, "How do people seeking asylum in the United Kingdom conceptualize and cope with the asylum journey?" (2020) Medicine, Conflict and Survival 2020, Vol. 36, No. 4, 333–358.

[2] Rebecca Yeo, "Disabled asylum seekers?...They don't really exist': The marginalisation of disabled asylum seekers in the UK and why it matters," (2015) Disability and the Global South, Vol. 2, No. 1, 523–550.

pandemic and for lessons for other similar organisations in the same field to learn from in case a similar event happens again.

This book will not directly compete with other similar books on the present market. To the best of my knowledge, I have not seen this type of research being conducted where staff are interviewed about their work with refugees and at such a pivotal time in the world's history coping with a pandemic whilst assisting a marginalised and vulnerable group within society. Therefore, this work is original in terms of its scope and provides an interesting perspective and narrative for the reader.

This book can be channelled towards the European and international academic learning environment market. Practitioners will be able to access the book to encourage wider knowledge and discussions on overlapping issues and themes associated with this book. Furthermore, it can be used as part of a relevant teaching module at any university and can be used in other modules by other academics across the world.

It can also be disseminated to third sector organisations who work with similar vulnerable groups to learn more about acquiring best practice which can be achieved because of an organisation working through the pandemic.

The themes of migration fit in closely with the United Nations Sustainable Development Goals (UNSDG)[3] as part of their 2030 Agenda outlining 17 goals encompassing the elimination of poverty and hunger, promoting health, education, gender equality, and reducing the impact of climate change amongst others.

The central thread linking migration to the UNSDG is seen through the advancement of States who should strive to promote peace, justice and strong institutions. The issue of migration is relevant here because they promotion of access to rights and processes within institutions to encourage equality and justice through a migration lens is crucial. Furthermore, whilst refugees are protected under specific International Law through the Refugee Convention, which is signed by most States, Goal 10 is pertinent here, advocating the reduction of inequality within and amongst countries which may facilitate a reason for people migrating in the first place from their country of origin and arriving in a host country. Specifically, Target 10.7 concerns the facilitation of "orderly,

---

[3] The United Nations General Assembly adopted the 2030 Agenda for Sustainable Development (2030 Agenda) in September 2015. The Agenda consists of 17 Sustainable Development Goals (SDGs).

safe, regular and responsible migration and mobility of people, including through the implementation of planned and well-managed migration policies."[4] As referenced:

> The characterization of 'well-managed migration policies' does not encompass the ultimate stage of refugees' travels, namely safe access to territory and to asylum procedures.[5]

This research is conducted within this anti-immigration environment and context, and how a third sector organisation addresses the many issues and challenges migrants experience given the excessive migrant flows in other continents which have availed themselves to Europe and the UK. Furthermore, the issue of migration is often connected to the risks associated with human trafficking and modern slavery. Therefore, the UNSDG refers to these overlapping issues including the "...Elimination all forms of violence against all women and girls in the public and private spheres, including trafficking and sexual and other types of exploitation,[6] taking immediate and effective measures to eradicate forced labour, end modern slavery and human trafficking and secure the prohibition and elimination of the worst forms of child labour, including recruitment and use of child soldiers, and by 2025 end child labour in all its forms,[7] ending abuse, exploitation, trafficking and all forms of violence and torture against children".[8]

This research also adopts a Constructivist Grounded Theory (CGT) which is a qualitative research method that involves co-constructing theories with participants. It is based on the theory that we all form views based on our own life experiences. As this work is multi-disciplinary, this approach is justified and used in many examples of social science research. The views of staff are heard within the research to give meaning to the work that they do and understand how their work impacts the lives of asylum seekers and refugees. It also is used as a means of reflection as

---

[4] Target 10.7 UN SDG.

[5] C. Denaro and M. Giuffre, "UN Sustainable Development Goals and the 'Refugee Gap': Leaving Refugees Behind?"(2022) Refugee Survey Quarterly, Vol. 41, 79–107 at 104.

[6] Target 5.2.

[7] Target 8.7.

[8] Target 16.2.

to their own emotions, feeling based on their experiences during the pandemic helping others. Similarly, the views and opinions of asylum seekers are included as they describe the impact that the pandemic had on them and the way they were still accommodated by staff during the social restrictions which were in place at that time.

The research will now examine the issues, challenges and barriers for frontline staff who work with asylum seekers by understanding how Covid-19 affected (either negatively or positively) their work with them. One third sector organisation was identified and agreed to provide lived experiences of their work. The research with asylum seekers and refugees includes the discussion of these issues with staff members and listening to those employees on the frontline with asylum seekers, refugees, victims of trafficking and smuggled persons to hear their experiences. It is important to understand how their work was carried out pre-Covid, how the lockdown restrictions impacted on their ability to continually work with victims effectively, and how their work has changed post Covid-19.

From a research aims and objectives perspective, the following questions will be answered:

1.What issues, challenges and barriers do frontline organisations working and supporting asylum seekers have in a politically toxic attitude to migrants?
2.How were these issues, challenges and barriers addressed pre-Covid, during Covid and after the pandemic?

3.How were these issues, challenges and barriers overcome?

4.What lessons can be learnt from the period pre-Covid, during Covid and post Covid to improve the working practices of organisations during their work helping and supporting asylum seekers and refugees?

This research will be anonymised and used as part of an impact piece of internationally published research. It is hoped that the research can be used across third sector environments to encourage best practice and improve the processes within frontline charities and organisations.

This project is most suited to being published as a Palgrave pivot title rather than a longer-form monograph or journal article because this is a specific and concise piece of research, focussing on narrow issues associated with the politically contentious issue of immigration and migration and how an organisation has operated within this environment during the pandemic. It is too large to be a journal article but too small to be considered a monograph.

A meeting between the researcher and the main contact from the front-line organisation took place outlining the main aims and objectives of the research. Upon the initial contact, participants were informed of all the parameters of the research project and their continuous right to withdraw from the project. This was done by requesting a consent form to be signed by each participant prior to the start of the interview. A base pool of participants was identified once a scheduled meeting with the main contact took place.

In addition to the doctrinal approach, the main methodology focussed on a qualitative method. During the qualitative research journey online interviews (MS Teams) took place using structured questions and semi structured questions where research participants were asked general questions about their role and responsibilities in the organisation and their views and opinions on the issues, challenges and barriers associated with their work. Unstructured questions were used to give the opportunity for participants to share their experiences of helping and supporting asylum seekers and refugees. The participants were from an organisation based in the UK but worked in various locations.

MS Teams links were sent directly to the research participant to ensure security. Research participants were in the lobby and not able to access the meeting without approval by way of admitting the participant into the meeting by the researcher. The interviews lasted between 45 and 60 minutes long. Once completed and recorded, the interviews were watched back, and transcripts read through to elicit content and testimony. An option of a second interview was available to facilitate more in-depth discussion on the content talked about in the first interviews.

Research participants were asked a series of specific questions and offered the opportunity to reflect on their role and responsibilities and consider how any processes in the organisation could be improved.

The interviews took place via MS Teams at a convenient time for both parties. Express permission allowing the meetings to be recorded was obtained from participants in advance in written form and at the start of each interview.

In terms of confidentiality, the study did require an extensive level of personal information (i.e. participants/contact details and locations). Participants are informed of this whilst being assured that any other information from them will only be used for this research and stored confidentiality.

Due to the sensitivity of the work participants are involved in, it is foreseeable that some participants did not wish to disclose certain aspects of their work. It may be too traumatic to talk about some aspects or examples of their work and therefore the research reflects this by omitting certain themes which may emotionally trigger some readers of this work.

Any identifiable information from the types of specific information which has been collated has been omitted. If there were any details which the participants do not wish to be quoted, this has not been included in the final published work.

Participants were informed and assured that the information from them will only be used for this research and stored confidentiality. All information has been treated with utmost confidentiality. Direct quotations from interviews have been fully anonymised. If information has been received which could identify any person involved in their work, the details were blacked out.

In addition, they were assured that participation in the interview was completely voluntary, and consent could be withdrawn at any time. At the end of the interview, participants consented to use the information was obtained during the interview and it was explained how it was to be used. The researcher did not disclose the locations of the frontline organisation to fully secure the safety and security of those involved in the research. There was no disclosure of the identities of people or service users.

Once the meetings took place, the interviews were uploaded and kept in a secure electronic folder which was only to be accessed by the researcher. Transcripts of the meetings were also available. At the end of the project all recorded meetings were deleted as they were no longer required for the research project. The listening and rewatching along with the writing up of the interviews took place in an environment away from other colleagues to secure confidentiality.

Research was conducted with staff members of the organisation using a qualitative design research method. Semi-structured interviews took place and discussed their experiences of working with asylum seekers and their views and opinions on the organisation. It is hoped that some of the recommendations will be implemented into existing and future policies of the organisation which will illustrate the impact of this research being carried out.

The organisation has requested to be anonymous throughout this research. References to the organisation will be referred to as 'AX.' AX is a charitable incorporated organisation (CIO) and a relatively new organisation. It lists its charitable objectives as the relief and assistance of people in need as victims of war, natural disasters or catastrophe. These objectives are reviewed by Trustees every year.

Their primary goal is the provision of direct aid and social support to displaced people. AX operates as an essentially volunteer run charity, which has roughly 1,000 volunteers in Europe and around 700 volunteers in the UK. The organisation is mostly funded by individual donations and organises big campaigns to encourage more donations. They do get some funding from trade unions and sometimes from grant awarding bodies. They deliver and provide frontline aid to support asylum seekers and refugees in the UK and two countries in the European Union (EU). As the charity has quickly expanded due to the needs of asylum seekers and refugees, it now employs 23 employed staff, including its CEO. The importance of volunteers cannot be underestimated and during the Winter, they can have roughly 35 volunteers who come to support activities at one location in Europe every day.

Part of their approach is to advocate for a fair and tolerant attitude towards refugees and protect asylum seekers with humanitarian supplies as they attempt to get to the UK to claim asylum. It is not uncommon for between 100 and 300 asylum seekers and refugees to attend distribution and service provisions a day at the largest location in Europe. Many asylum seekers are from Northern Africa, Afghanistan and the Middle East, fleeing persecution and in need of humanitarian aid. AX supported several people from Afghanistan who fought alongside the British and American forces as part of the US-led Operation Enduring Freedom (OEF) between 2003 and 2014. It has also assisted and supported refugees from Ukraine after the invasion by Russia. Despite many displaced persons claiming refuge in Europe, an objective for some is to get to the UK to submit a claim for refugee status. For many they can speak English as well as a second language and have friends and family connections already in the UK. Also, there is a perception that the UK is a safe and welcoming place, a more tolerant country than other parts of Europe, and a country which upholds human rights.

The European operation makes many provisions including warm bedding, shoes and clothing, toiletries, food and hot drinks and medical supplies. Other services include hairdressing, bike repairs and phone charging. In addition, providing social support is part of their objectives. During the afternoons staff and volunteers spend time in communities. This involves organising workshops and language lessons to negate social isolation and alienation. In the UK, advocacy is also a large part of their work, pressuring the change in Government policies hostile to migrants and asylum seekers. This involves hosting campaigns to create awareness of these issues and push for change as to how asylum seekers and refugees are treated so that they are welcomed more positively in the UK. This has been evidenced from the opposition to the Rwanda policy which seeks to deport asylum seekers from the UK to have their claims processed abroad. Moreover, they have advocated for the plight of asylum seekers and refugees because of the detrimental impact the Nationality and Borders Act 2022 and the Illegal Migration Act 2023 has had on this vulnerable group. The UK operation focusses on clothing, activities (including English lessons, trips, social activities) and guidance/advice.

The numbers of asylum seekers who are present where the organisation exists is not constant, they fluctuate a lot. There are always people there. AX see more service users during the summer than in the winter as many asylum seekers take advantage of the better weather by travelling across the Mediterranean across the Balkan region to get to where the organisation is based, but the need for support tends to be much greater in the Winter (from the need for coats to mental health support). There are approximately 700 asylum seekers and refugees at one of the locations where AX is helping on the frontline in their European operation. Staff and volunteers report that they see a lot of death and hear about the abuse and trauma which asylum seekers have experienced which is never really acknowledged or highlighted in the media. They also hear about asylum seekers' talk about their past lives and experiences. Many asylum seekers are Syrian and from Eritrea, so it is not uncommon for staff and volunteers to be shown pictures asylum seekers have of their houses and families they have left behind. Their experiences educate AX of the stories of persecution experienced with some leaving behind good jobs and careers:

> They tell you their jobs they had…you speak to a lot of engineers, doctors, teachers who tend to be more middle-class in the countries they have come from.[9]

[9] Participant B3.

Staff and volunteers also hear how conscription of young children has taken place which made many people from Eritrea and Sudan flee to Europe:

> We see a large number of people from Eritrea and Sudan because of enforced conscription. Those are often younger men, who are being recruited to fight. They are the ones being targeted into these armies. So, they are different to Syrian asylum seekers as they have less money and less means.[10]

Often in the European operation the living conditions are very poor and asylum seekers are subjected to hostility from the police such as having their sleeping bags and personal possessions confiscated. Tents and shelters are often dismantled so they cannot shield from the elements. The research will illustrate the impact of the wet weather on the already poor living conditions and the challenges AX faced.

Asylum seekers are subjected to poor living conditions, unable to change their clothes and susceptible to skin diseases as access to sanitation is limited. Consequently, poor health combined with a lack of sleep creates numerous health issues. AX work with a group of UK healthcare professionals who travel to the EU to triage asylum seekers, provide emergency healthcare, prescribe medication and first aid care.

As well as European operations, the charity set up a UK presence during the pandemic to run operations from various parts of the UK. Primarily, it is an organisation where their operations are in person (i.e. run by volunteers) but their staff are remote. Volunteers conduct most of their activities face to face, with some volunteer meetings also in person. However, their larger meetings with volunteer leads from across the country will be online. It does not have a UK office but rather they have groups all over the country. Any meetings with volunteer teams take place online and illustrate a virtual persona as to how it operates.

AX staff and volunteers assist asylum seekers in the UK whilst they are waiting to hear from the Home Office about their claims for asylum being accepted or not. Due to the low supply of housing resulting in the Government's policy of dispersing asylum seekers across towns and cities within the UK, thousands of asylum seekers have been housed in temporary accommodation in hotels and B&B accommodation. Despite not

[10] Participant B3.

assisting any people in B&B accommodation, AX presently helps approximately 3,500 asylum seekers at over 40 hotels and have advocated for improving the poor living standards in accommodation of asylum seekers. In the same way as they help people in Europe, they provide essential clothing to UK-based asylum seekers whilst providing help on health. They do not provide legal or immigration advice, given that these are professional services and regulated areas. As there is little to no support to asylum seekers and refugees, the thought of navigating their way through the UK's immigration system can often be a daunting prospect and overwhelming experience. AX assist by providing access to interpreters, gather and collect paperwork, signpost to over 40 firms of solicitors and liaise with their legal representatives. They also provide emotional and social support to manage the waits in receiving a decision from the Home Office because of the significant backlog in processing claims.[11]

Additionally, they help with refugees getting registered with doctors and other healthcare professionals. As some refugees are part of families with small children, AX helps young refugees into school.

A desk-based review of the challenges for asylum seekers entering the UK from the EU alongside the procedural and social issues which faced them when they were in the UK because of the UK asylum system took place. The numerous first-hand accounts of the lived experiences and how they played out during the pandemic give a fascinating insight into how the organisation has evolved during this period which has significantly impacted the help and support provided to asylum seekers and refugees. Post-pandemic, the research provides a reflective account of how their advocacy and work continues to be directed by Government policies.

The semi structured interviews took place with staff between November and December 2023. Here are the results of the interviews which provide a greater insight into their work and explain their experiences of working during Covid-19 and afterwards, post-pandemic.

---

[11] This was particularly relevant when the Home Office introduced a streamlined version of the asylum questionnaire in 2022 which was offered to individuals from Afghanistan, Eritrea, Syria, Yemen, and Libya who claimed asylum before 28 June 2022. This was introduced to address the significant backlogs in the asylum process system. As 95% of those individuals from the nationalities above were given a positive decision, this is why the fast-track questionnaire was introduced.

# CHAPTER 3

# The Structure of the Organisation

**Abstract** This chapter highlights how many charities and organisations go about their work to fulfil their aims and functions together with their obligations towards assisting and supporting asylum seekers and refugees are seldom reported. The use of social media within their work has been seen to demonstrate how effective this tool can be to create awareness to society and as it is a charity, it provides a channel for people to contribute funds to support the work they do. The role of the media in dictating agendas in issues associated with immigration is also referred to in this chapter. The chapter emphasises the importance of experience and knowledge of the employees and what qualities they bring to the organisation to support refugees. The issue of immigration is often politically charged and therefore the organisation works within a very challenging social and political environment, and this is explained in the chapter alongside explaining the impact this has on how they carry out their functions. The chapter ends by explaining the importance of volunteers within the organisation and the significant role they play in the organisation fulfilling its aims and objectives as a charity for the benefit of asylum seekers and refugees.

**Keywords** Hostile Environment Policy · Brexit · Impact on Trafficked Victims

© The Author(s), under exclusive license to Springer Nature Switzerland AG 2025
M. Davis, *Third Sector Organisations, Asylum Seekers and Refugees,*
https://doi.org/10.1007/978-3-031-85137-7_3

The following chapters examine what was found from the interviews conducted. The testimony provides an honest and transparent account of what staff experienced during the pandemic and how they addressed the issues the pandemic threw at them. It explains what the challenges for asylum seekers were during this time before moving on to what these issues are post-pandemic. Staff explain what the benefits of working for the organisation are and how they presently cope given the issues and barriers their work exist within. Within this section there are recommendations as to what improvement X could make for the benefit of staff, volunteers, asylum seekers, refugees and for the organisation. It is hoped that some of the suggestions are acted upon by AX which will show the impact of this research being undertaken.

The priority of AX is to provide humanitarian support to asylum seekers and refugees. This assistance fills the gap in provision which is not provided by the State and consequently exposes individuals to violations of their human rights with regard to fulfilling a good social and economic life.[1] For staff this is why the organisation exists, as "it is about the individuals we support providing as much humanity as we can because the situation is dehumanising."[2]

There is no question that the organisation hires very well experienced staff within their workforce who are ideally trained in working with asylum seekers and supporting staff members and volunteers. Combined with this there is a large draw for people to want to work for AX because of the opportunity it offers to work closely on the frontline with refugees, with many staff having a desire to help and support asylum seekers. There is no doubt that asylum seekers and refugees are a vulnerable social group who deserve protection and support from society. There is a need for this work and evidences a further reason why AX attracts a certain type of person to work for them. An additional reason for joining was to challenge the government's policies which affect migrants, asylum seekers and refugees:

> Not that I voted for this government, it's in my name and it's the policies which are from the UK government, so to be able to work here and try

---

[1] Article 25 of the Universal Declaration of Human Rights, United Nations General Assembly in Paris on 10 December 1948—General Assembly resolution 217 A.

[2] Participant B3.

to challenge those policies through the solidarity of the work that we do is very important to me.[3]

AX has a strong social media presence which is used very effectively. It has accounts on Twitter, Facebook and Instagram. Much of the sign-posting for enquiries for help flow through these channels alongside requests to give donations by the public and other organisations. Most of the donations come from UK donors. For many asylum seekers, AX is the first point of contact they connect with to get help and support. Therefore, the monitoring of these social media channels requires significant time and investment from staff to maintain. A common situation of how an asylum seeker reaches out for help occurs in the following way:

> ...we get a lot of enquiries through Facebook and Instagram from asylum seekers who maybe have that. And from that I'll put them in touch directly with our teams or signpost them into the direction that they need, whether we can help or not.[4]

One of the many qualities staff bring to AX is their knowledge and experience of working with individuals from other vulnerable groups. One staff member had specific knowledge of the UK asylum system and how it works in practice. This is instrumental to understanding what asylum seekers must navigate as part of the asylum process:

> Claiming all the way up to receiving their status or not, and the processes involved all the way through interviews and residence permits, and then once getting status, kind of the obstacles then or what needs to happen in order for someone to move into a property...I already had that overview and therefore I was aware of the difficulties and challenges and the areas where people need support.[5]

AX work in a very challenging social and political environment and often the work which is done by the organisation is both challenging and rewarding at the same time. Nevertheless, staff and volunteers are often subjected to the risk of intimidation especially in situations where

---

[3] Participant B3.

[4] Participant B2.

[5] Participant B2.

demonstrations are held such as the temporary housing of asylum seekers in hotels. One such incident took place in the UK where there was a protest outside a hotel and the organisation was there.

The media plays a large part in dictating the agenda associated with immigration issues in the UK. Staff report that "...if something is in the news that obviously heightens peoples' tensions and anxieties which brings out the far right, it doesn't always help the situation."[6] The workload of staff increases in waves when something has been in the news. Consequently, the media plays an influential role in driving the agenda against foreign nationals which part of the electorate attach their opinions and actions against asylum seekers. This undoubtably has issues for staff and volunteers who expect a duty of care from their employer whilst being involved in this work. The safeguarding of service users is paramount. Safeguarding issues are referred to managers as a process of escalation within the organisation who have specific interviewing and practice experience in this area:

> I'm aware of safeguarding procedures relating to that and how important that is and alerting the relevant people, or if I'm speaking to people for interview purposes, the sensitivity needed with that and the importance of it.[7]

This research looks at the important role volunteers play in the organisation. It is not uncommon for paid staff members to have started work with AX as a volunteer first. One staff member "was a volunteer for 18 months with one of the groups. I was one of our lead volunteers. And yeah, from that I sort of stepped into a full-time position."[8] AX benefits from having a dynamic workforce with staff able to see the benefits of volunteering and having certain experiences as a volunteer which then can be transferred into policies which can be suggested and implemented by the same staff member in a paid position. This uniqueness of the workforce is extremely beneficial as employees can appreciate both perspectives, one from being a volunteer and then the other by becoming a paid staff member.

---

[6] Participant B6.

[7] Participant B2.

[8] Participant B1.

Staff recognise how hostile the political environment is whilst working for the benefit of asylum seekers and refugees. This has continued to be facilitated by the Nationality & Borders Act 2022, the Illegal Migration Act 2023 and the continued litigation surrounding the Rwanda policy. It was stated that "this kind of thing links to the hostile environment."[9]

The organisation has a new CEO who joined in May 2023. This led to more policies being put in place for staff and volunteers. It has been reported that before the change of leadership there "was a huge amount of turbulence and confusion as to what is it that we're actually doing."[10] There also had previously been concerns that "there was not much structure and lone working without the connection of working in a team."[11] Since the change of CEO, staff reported that there is now more structure and additional policies in place.

Staff are engaged with progressing with the development of their services and as these took shape especially in the UK, more policies were implemented. As the charity continues to expand there is "a hope for new roles to be created and for people to move around and take on other tasks and responsibilities."[12] However, what this will look like is yet to be seen.

Staff explained that the induction at the start of their employment takes place online. As there is no central office of operations, this method sounded extremely practical. As well as training on the UK asylum system, staff also have mandatory sessions to complete:

> ...you do a safeguarding training session and then we have mandated training. I think it has changed in the last few months, but we have training that is all online training. It's like a zoom call where we have a presentation and go through scenarios, then training on distributions and simulating problems which come up and how to resolve them.[13]

However, a different employee explained that their experience of induction was very different. Although the employee was given a job description, there was some confusion as to what lengths employees and volunteers should go to in their work, and how things should be done

---

[9] Participant B1.

[10] Participant B6.

[11] Participant B5.

[12] Participant B2.

[13] Participant B1.

in line with expectations of the organisation. For example, the employee queried how asylum seekers were expected to get from point A to point B to access a provided service. The question from the employee was, "Can I drive them? And the response was, I don't know."[14] Once the online training has been completed, the organisation works on a hybrid basis where remote working takes place alongside visits to groups and teams of volunteers. As admitted, the limits of online working are evidenced:

> We have a lot of meetings online, it's hard to bring a big group of people together in an online meeting to all chat about things. So, I think it is something which we're trying to sort of address a bit more, more meetings and more connection between groups. Often, we won't know what the legal access team is doing because we just don't talk to them as much. So, I think that's the main sort of problem with being online.[15]

Highlighting and implementing best practices are important in any organisation. AX advocates this approach by "having monthly meetings with hotel leads and the regional leads. And that's where best practice will be shared, and people bring up any issues they've faced."[16]

One of the many roles which staff play is to empower their volunteers. One participant explained that for her, "empowering volunteers to let them know that what is being done is helping here is really important."[17] A deeper discussion of the valued contribution volunteers make to the lives of asylum seekers and refugees will now take place.

It is clear the positive impact volunteers have on the organisation and the way in which they contribute to AX's aims and objectives as a humanitarian charity. It was stressed that "without the help from volunteers we could not do as much as we could, and they play a significant part."[18] There are several ways volunteers assist asylum seekers. They assist with language difficulties and learning to speak English along with signposting people to signposting people to local services and help with distributing aid and providing a place of solidarity and support. When asylum seekers

---

[14] Participant B6.
[15] Participant B1.
[16] Participant B1.
[17] Participant B6.
[18] Participant B3.

become refugees, volunteers offer support to claim benefits and speak with local housing teams to get adequate accommodation.

The quality of volunteers AX can call upon to provide in-person support is not in question and demonstrates a great ethos which volunteers buy into:

> They are so dedicated to AX...sometimes I forget that they have a full-time job and yet they are so quick to respond to requests. They're so knowledgeable, they're like real experts in their field and yet they're volunteers, and it is incredible. We are lucky to have a long running core group of volunteers to rely on.[19]

This is incredibly impressive and also considering that there is a specific group of volunteers who are classed as 'virtual volunteers' who can be asked to provide a specific service by a staff member virtually. Every volunteer brings their own level of energy and experience to the role. This creates a positive identity within the organisation. It was reported that AX in their European operation have roughly 35 volunteers helping daily during the winter when the interviews took place. In addition, the UK operation has hundreds of volunteers working in different groups across the UK. Interestingly, during the pandemic they saw many more international volunteers travel to volunteer:

> During the Covid-19 pandemic we saw an increase in volunteers across Europe as it was much easier to travel to Europe than UK volunteers travelling to Europe. We saw volunteers from France, Germany, Netherlands, and Spain. We now have a couple of Australians now who are in Europe travelling working and a few from the USA.[20]

There seems to be a greater awareness of the issues involved in immigration by volunteers who give their time and contribute to making the lives of asylum seekers better. More broadly, there is a huge interest in the issues affecting asylum seekers and refugees and the need for more to be done to help and support them. As AX is regarded as being outspoken and an advocacy organisation, this gives them the ability to attract new volunteers as one staff member highlights:

[19] Participant B2.
[20] Participant B3.

I just moved to London, and I wanted to get involved with some projects in the local community. I think the specific issue of refugees and asylum seekers is something that I studies when I was at university, and it was big in the news at the time. Then I heard about AX quite a lot, I knew that they were quite vocal in the media. And they're outspoken. And I quite like that about them as an organisation. So that is why I chose to go with them in the first place.[21]

AX has registered many international volunteers who have moved to the UK and volunteered. Many of these are students enrolled in university courses. One big advantage of having volunteers from different countries is their ability to assist with many languages of asylum seekers and the ability to help asylum seekers and refugees adjust to living in the UK. Some volunteers in their European operation choose to work for weeks or months at a time and during the summer AX report that they see a large contingent of university students. The UK operation has many volunteers who tend to be long-term volunteers, but often volunteer alongside work and study.

As well as students and international volunteers, AX have very strong links with unions including the National Education Union and the Fire Brigade Union. Each send delegations of volunteers over to Europe during weekends. Volunteers are a broad mix of genders and ages:

We have a younger people in their 20's, but also quite a lot of people who are retired and some older volunteers.[22]

There are more females than males in younger age groups but within the older volunteer community, the ages are much more evenly spread across genders. What is interesting is that some volunteers are more time rich, rather than cash rich:

A lot of people interested in humanitarian aid come because they have the time to give, so they may not be cash rich, but they are time rich. Weekend volunteers tend to be slightly older, and they may be at work during the weekends.[23]

---

[21] Participant B1.

[22] Participant B1.

[23] Participant B3.

Within the demographic of volunteers, many are of a white ethnic origin. AX has volunteers who have lived experience and have extensive knowledge which they can pass on to the organisation. As many asylum seekers and refugees are identified as a non-white ethnicity, AX is very welcoming to people who can contribute to their work in this way. AX is trying to encourage more people from similar ethnic origin groups as their service users and people with lived experience as refugees to become part of the organisation to continue contributing to the work for the benefit of people they are supporting:

> This is an important perspective for us to acknowledge and as we mature, I think it is something we'll look to focus on more as well as having refugee voices being heard and advocated from within AX.[24]

The next section looks at the specific issues, barriers and challenges staff and volunteers experienced during the Covid-19 pandemic. It will also highlight the difficulties asylum seekers experienced during Covid-19 from the lens of staff. The following section provides a fascinating insight as to how AX adapted well given the restrictions that the pandemic placed on civil society affecting asylum seekers and refugees.

---

[24] Participant B1.

# CHAPTER 4

# The Issues for Staff and Volunteers and the Organisation During the Covid-19 Pandemic

**Abstract** This chapter examines the specific issues, barriers and challenges staff and volunteers experienced during the Covid-19 pandemic. It highlights the difficulties asylum seekers experienced from the perspective of employed staff who provide a fascinating insight into the situations they were faced with and the impact on asylum seekers and refugees. It provides a comprehensive insight into how leaders and managers of the organisation had to adapt to the restrictions which the pandemic imposed on society which then affected how they could continue the support provided to asylum seekers and refugees.

**Keywords** Nationality & Borders Act 2022 · Illegal Migration Act 2023 · Disqualifications from protection · Temporary permission to stay for trafficked victims

There was no question that there was an enormous effort and conscientiousness of volunteers during the pandemic. One of the examples was when the social restrictions were imposed on society, but asylum seekers and refugees still required assistance when the policy of the Government was to house many migrants in hotels. The combination of the social restrictions with the logistical issues the pandemic posed made it hard for volunteers to get to the hotels to help support asylum seekers, but this is when the need for support was identified by the organisation and began. It was very difficult to communicate and reach out to asylum seekers and refugees during this time. This frustrated many volunteers as they perceived that they were not able to help as much as they would have liked. A staff member believed that "we should have given more consideration to the impact of mental health of volunteers regards their well-being with stronger boundaries and guidelines established."[1] Not only did the societal restrictions have an impact on staff, but they also had a detrimental impact on the mental health of asylum seekers during this time:

> I think as well in terms of the people that we support, asylum seekers living in hotels, I think their lives were more difficult during lockdown because they were locked down in hotels and in small hotel rooms with not much if anything to do.[2]

Before the emergence of Covid-19, Organisation AX had one operation which was based solely in Europe. The pandemic fundamentally altered the way in which the organisation functioned with the opening of a UK operation at the end of 2020. This was a significant change—as stated above prior to 2020 AX just had one operation but the pandemic resulted in the need for the UK to also have an operation based on the need of asylum seekers and refugees who as a marginalised group prior to the pandemic required even more assistance during the pandemic. Furthermore, the pandemic resulted in less people donating to causes and charities. There was a disconnection between the individual and society which often meant that the awareness of social issues and communications became somewhat limited. The online and remote-led workforce (i.e. the UK staff team) did not exist until late 2020. The European operation had always been in-person and continued to be during and after the pandemic. Despite AX adding an online and remote-led workforce to their overall support operation in the UK, this approach was severely tested during this time. Organisation AX did not become remote because of Covid, they literally did not exist in the UK before, and had no presence whatsoever. Consequently, not all the new staff were prepared for such change so early on in their careers with the AX:

---

[1] Participant B1.

[2] Participant B1.

Everyone was very supportive and welcoming me to the team and I just picked up what I needed to do quite quickly and kind of realised that. It's a completely remote role and so even though I was in touch with the team online, it was an adjustment which needed to be made.[3]

Furthermore, a big disadvantage to some UK staff during the pandemic was the loss or inability to interact with other staff because there was in-person office. All staff in the UK operation have always worked remotely, although UK staff do visit in-person groups. The European operation is the only operation where staff are present on site. Staff had to be more independent which some employees found more difficult than others:

> For me the adjustment was getting used to not being around people and learning from people just by being around them in an office situation. It's a lot more independently driven, you know, putting meetings in place, reaching out to people, to ask questions rather than having them close by and learning from them that way.[4]

Warehouse and office space was more readily available during the pandemic as local councils and authorities were restricting many employees from being in work with the Government imposing social restrictions which impacted the ability for any employees to attend locations of employment. This was because people were not renting spaces and so they were empty, and so there were opportunities to use them for at a reduced rent or for free. However, AX did not use any warehouse space in the course of their work helping migrants. Post-pandemic, the situation regarding the availability of space became a very different story:

> When the pandemic eased then we started losing these spaces which meant that we really struggled to find spaces for distributions, especially in places like London. Local council support which was there during the worst times of the pandemic suddenly disappeared because the Council simply did not have the funding anymore for that.[5]

---

[3] Participant B2.

[4] Participant B2.

[5] Participant B5.

Whilst most countries had weaker social restrictions placed upon them by their governments, some States had stricter social controls. This made it either impossible or at best very difficult for volunteers to leave the UK and travel to the European country where AX was operating. There was an increased police presence at the European operation AX were working at, but not at UK accommodation sites:

> During that time the police was very present, obviously because they were looking for people who were not sticking to the Covid rules, the curfew and the lockdown.[6]

In the UK most of the work was done inside at hotels or local community centres, mosques, churches, etc. Humanitarian aid delivery was an exception to the observance and enforcement of social restrictions. For those volunteers and staff working in the European operation during the pandemic, they were able to continue their work to some extent by working outdoors by wearing PPE[7]:

> Despite most of our work being outside, we had very strict protocols for wearing masks. We were wearing one FFP2 mask and then a disposable mask over the top. This was important because we used to see 300 people attend each of our distribution and service provisions.[8]

AX also altered the way in which they worked by providing aid in a socially distanced way:

> We introduced socially distanced distributions, which is as ridiculous as it sounds, but we usually have people join at the back of the back of our van. So, we would put cones down about 1 metre or two metres apart from each other.[9]

In the European operation, there was no food provision provided by authorities during the pandemic because of the social restrictions. People

---

[6] Participant B3.

[7] Personal Protective Equipment such as gloves and face masks.

[8] Participant B3.

[9] Participant B3.

seeking asylum in the UK who were in receipt of Sect. 95 support[10] continued to be provided with food in hotels. AX started a socially distanced food provision distribution service during this time. The three priorities of the organisation during this time were 1) the health and welfare of asylum seekers, 2) not breaching the Covid rules of that country which occasionally altered from time to time from being eased to being reintroduced, and 3) protecting the volunteers from the virus. At times, it was stated that this was difficult:

> It was quite difficult to interpret the two different countries and we wanted to make sure that we were being as cautious as possible for the communities that we supported, because access to medical care is not very well provided for refugees.[11]

The organisation in Europe primarily worked outside which meant that the more asylum seekers could be supported rather than being subjected to restricted numbers as the case would be helping people indoors. The UK operation did not start until 2020 and did initially start some work (e.g. clothing distributions) outside due to social distancing. However, as the research later demonstrates, staff and volunteers were subjected to very poor weather conditions at times which hampered their operations. The country where AX was one of the many countries which had police enforce social distancing and maintain restrictions very tightly. There was a curfew imposed between the hours of 6pm and 6am where no citizens were allowed to leave their house under any circumstances without a form explaining why you had to leave:

> We had a small but very long-term group of volunteers, and we found that they were subject to very strict rules and paperwork. We had to fill out a form to come to the warehouse in the morning, a form in the afternoon to go out to distribution aid centres and a different form to go home again

---

[10] The Home Office is under a legal obligation under Sect. 95 Immigration and Asylum Act 1999 to provide housing and financial support to a person who is seeking asylum and is destitute and awaiting a decision from them on their claim for asylum. Support will continue until the person's asylum claim is finally determined by the Home Office or appeal courts.

[11] Participant B3.

in the evening. We were consistently subjected to ID checks, maybe 3 or 4 times a week we would have the police arrive at our distribution sites.[12]

As stated above the fact that humanitarian aid delivery was an exception to the restriction rules. AX was able to provide forms for volunteers and staff to explain their work and not subject to the societal restrictions. These were particularly useful as staff and volunteers were pulled over by the police to have their ID and forms checked.

When social restrictions started to ease, AX found that there was more interest in people from the UK to travel to work for them because their financial and social situations had changed because of the pandemic:

> They'd lost their jobs or were on furlough, so they were in a position to give their time quite freely, accommodation in the country was very cheap because no one was travelling here for holidays.[13]

A difficult challenge operating through the pandemic was the frequent changes to government health and pandemic guidance, outlining what restrictions were being eased and which activities continued to be prohibited:

> I think it was around April 2021, the UK threatened to put the country where we were working on the Red List. And so, a lot of our volunteers left. Around Christmas 2020 and Christmas 2021 there was a two-week isolation period imposed on volunteers travelling from the UK. Obviously, this impacted on our numbers of volunteers as they were put off by this regulation.[14]

One of the benefits which arose during the pandemic was when testing kits became available to staff and volunteers. Prior to this there was no testing of asylum seekers or refugees by the authorities as they are not eligible under the social security or healthcare system. The testing regime helped staff and volunteers test for the virus and in cases of positive results they could isolate staff in the usual way:

---

[12] Participant B3.

[13] Participant B3.

[14] Participant B3.

Basically, we had a system where if someone had symptoms, they were sent to be tested. We had one outbreak in December 2020 amongst the volunteers and once that happened, we ceased some operations for the day to make sure everyone could get tested to make sure that we then had no Covid.[15]

Furthermore, once the vaccination programme was rolled out, AX requested that all volunteers have the vaccine and made it a mandatory requirement to continue work or to start work with them. In the European country where AX was based, asylum seekers and refugees were not allowed access to vaccinations because they are a group who sit outside of State support although prior to the pandemic the Red Cross did try and implement a vaccination programme. In the UK, the position was more advantageous because they could be allowed access to the NHS, which includes the provision of vaccines. Asylum seekers were reluctant to have the vaccine even if they were offered one due to mistrust of authorities and as their intention was to get to the UK, some would say that they would have it there instead:

A lot of people here also think that they will only be here for a few days and then they will cross to the UK. In fact, people are here for much longer, but they were saying, well I'll get a vaccination when I go to the UK or, you know, like if the UK offers me one, I'll take it.[16]

Staff and volunteers found that the police were not hostile to them. In contrast, the behaviour of police to asylum seekers and refugees was more hostile. Staff reported that the police made life difficult for asylum seekers by constantly moving them on to other places where they had set up basic shelters. It was not clear whether this has always been the case with the police or due to the impact of the pandemic which made the police more observant of the activities of the organisation with their support provision to asylum seekers.

---

[15] Participant B3.
[16] Participant B3.

# CHAPTER 5

# The Issues for Asylum Seekers DURING the Covid-19 Pandemic

**Abstract** There has been very literature written or research undertaken as to the impact the pandemic had on asylum seekers and refugees obtaining assistance and support during Covid-19. As a marginalised group, they found themselves outside the usual protection support afforded to them by governments as a direct response to the pandemic. This chapter focusses exclusively on the impact the pandemic had on asylum seekers and refugees. It considers the government response to the pandemic which implemented a policy of housing migrants in temporary accommodation and the physical and mental health impacts on them. The chapter discusses the important role staff and volunteers played during this period to keep supporting asylum seekers and the methods of how they achieved this whilst asylum seekers waited to hear about their asylum claims from the Home Office.

**Keywords** Human Trafficking · Exploitation · Human Rights · Covid-19 · Pandemic · Identification

Despite the pandemic having an effect of reducing the number of migrants in the world by 2 million people,[1] the experiences from AX suggest that the pandemic had little impact on refugees travelling during this period:

> During the Summer we see many more people than we do in the Winter and that is because the weather is much better. But I'd say that the pandemic had very little impact on people travelling to seek asylum from my experience.[2]

During the pandemic, the UK government accommodated asylum seekers in UK hotels to prevent them from being homeless due to the closing of some local authority housing teams.[3] This was explained as a temporary measure, but it is important to point out that the Government has continued to use hotel accommodation, and so it cannot be regarded as a temporary measure. As there has been a large backlog of asylum cases waiting to be processed by the Home Office to be communicated to asylum seekers, hotels were used as a method of accommodating them due to no local authority housing stock provision being available. Coincidentally, more hotels were opened to approximately 9,500 asylum seekers during the pandemic.[4] AX found that many people, especially single men were being moved from hotel to hotel during the pandemic and then when the pandemic ended, the policy changed:

> Recently, they have been trying to close the hotels now that we are on the other side of it. We have one of the hotels in Crystal Palace in South London but are moving all the single men from that hotel to one at Heathrow.[5]

---

[1] International Organization for Migration (IOM), "The Impacts of COVID-19 on Migration and Migrants from a Gender Perspective," IOM, Geneva, 2022 at Xi, accessed at https://publications.iom.int/system/files/pdf/impacts-of-COVID-19-gender_1.pdf.

[2] Participant B3.

[3] See Home Office News, "The use of temporary hotels to house asylum seekers during Covid-19," 8 August 2020, accessed at https://homeofficemedia.blog.gov.uk/2020/08/08/the-use-of-temporary-hotels-to-house-asylum-seekers-during-covid-19/.

[4] Melanie Gower, "Asylum accommodation: hotels, vessels and large-scale sites," House of Commons Library, Research Briefing, 7 July 2023 at 4.

[5] Participant B1.

Since the lifting of restrictions, the Government has tried to close some hotels to cut costs. Not many hotels have closed unless the Government has done so to try to cut costs for political reasons to show the electorate that they have been reducing the amount spent on tackling the asylum issue in the UK. Despite asylum seekers being moved during the pandemic they were still subjected to the same societal restrictions as other citizens. The imposed social restrictions heavily impacted asylum seekers due to isolation:

> I think that in terms of the people that we support, asylum seekers living in the hotels. I think their lives were more difficult during lockdown because they were locked down in hotels and in very small rooms with nothing to do.[6]

Mental health concerns of asylum seekers were a significant issue during this period due to inactivity and restrictions which compounded their previous experiences of trauma:

> People felt low and down because there was not much in the way of activity and people felt trapped in their hotel rooms. A lot of people who had come to the UK have already experienced a lot of trauma and the isolation element did not help in engaging activities in the community.[7]

There is a nexus between the impact of trauma and how this can often lead to vulnerability of certain individuals of at-risk groups who require support. This idea of trauma occurring in the case of someone fleeing their own country creates vulnerability from the outset which exposes them to a risk of further trauma at different stages of someone's life. It has been reported that staff expressed how many asylum seekers were experiencing a lot of loss during the period and that Covid-19 represented a further type of loss which makes them even more vulnerable:

> Even when there was just so much loss during Covid-19 there was a huge amount of loss before Covid-19 with many people fleeing countries and families being left behind. There was a steady stream of loss that created

---

[6] Participant B1.

[7] Participant B5.

vulnerabilities akin to asylum seekers who were marginalised due to them not having access to help and support.[8]

Often asylum seekers would be sharing facilities and rooms with strangers which was disconcerting, many of which did not speak the same language, making communication difficult:

> On top of any situation where people may feel isolated, they were sharing accommodation with strangers and people who were speaking different languages, and they are away from home.[9]

Many asylum seekers were compromised by not being able to communicate with staff because AX could not reach people to get them enough data on their phones to communicate with those they were supporting. As well as phone calls being difficult, many staff and volunteers relied on public transport. When public transport was not available, asylum seekers were left without assistance and support for long periods.

Isolation became very problematic and a regular theme for many asylum seekers during this period. As many were progressing through the asylum process which involves a lot of waiting for decisions,[10] many people felt alienated from the process because of the impact the lockdown had on their claims not being decided in timeframes they were expecting and expressed a feeling of limbo[11]:

> The fact that there is a backlog of cases and so more people having to be accommodated for longer meant that many had to be housed in hotels. They are having to wait so long for their claims to be heard. They felt

---

[8] Participant B6.

[9] Participant B2.

[10] Figures show that of the roughly 14,500 applications that received an initial decision in 2021, 4% received their decision within 6 months, 19% within a year, and 53% took at least 1.5 years to receive an initial Home Office decision. See 'The UK's asylum backlog,' Migration Observatory Research, 5 April 2023 accessed at https://migrationobservatory.ox.ac.uk/resources/briefings/the-uks-asylum-backlog/.

[11] In March 2021 over 50,000 had been waiting for an initial decision for more than 6 months, again, the highest for over a decade. See Andy Hewett, "Living in Limbo: A decade of delays in the UK asylum system," July 2021 at 1, accessed at https://www.refugeecouncil.org.uk/wp-content/uploads/2021/07/Living-in-Limbo-A-decade-of-delays-in-the-UK-Asylum-system-July-2021.pdf.

alienated and so more mental health pressures started to start or build up during that period because of the gap in contact to some extent.[12]

However, asylum seekers remained optimistic that their lives will get better once they receive their positive asylum decisions. Moreover, the reality is that once asylum seekers receive positive decisions, they become refugees and are exposed to new challenges as refugees, different to those encountered as asylum seekers, but often the perspectives from asylum seekers is usually the opposite:

> There's a feeling of well 've been living in a hotel for two years, that wasn't great. So now that I've got refugee status, I'll be able to move to something better. The Council will provide me with better accommodation and that is the sort of belief that lots of people have. That isn't the case.[13]

Where refugees receive a positive decision from their application to claim asylum, they have 28 days to find alternative accommodation.[14] Therefore, AX find themselves having to manage the expectations of asylum seekers but do not downplay the positive perspective some migrants have of the UK, they try to provide the best information and guidance possible to help people with the move-on process and avoid homelessness.

In contrast to the situation in the UK where asylum seekers were housed in hotels during the period, many people who AX were supporting in the European location during the pandemic were living outside in tents:

> So, the idea was that the people living on the streets had no fixed abode and therefore were not subject to the same COVID-19 regulations, whereas in the UK we saw people who were living on the street and homeless were given hotel accommodation.[15]

---

[12] Participant B1.

[13] Participant B1.

[14] Home Office, "Ceasing Sect. 95 Support instruction," Version 2.0, 7 July 2023, accessed at https://assets.publishing.service.gov.uk/media/64afb2fe8bc29f000d2ccc78/Ceasing_Section_95_Support_Instruction.pdf.

[15] Participant B3.

The issues discussed above including mental health, isolation, access to services and accommodation were prevalent to asylum seekers prior to the pandemic. However, these same issues were exacerbated during the pandemic. The severity of their issues increased because of the impact of the pandemic on society and how individuals and communities as well as organisations withdrew from participation in society during this time. The next section identifies and examines the issues asylum seekers had after the pandemic in more detail.

# CHAPTER 6

# The Issues for Asylum Seekers AFTER the Covid-19 Pandemic

**Abstract** Many vulnerable individuals from marginalised groups were negatively impacted during the pandemic, and when social restrictions lifted after the severity of the pandemic started to reduce, many asylum seekers found themselves with new challenges to overcome to be recognised as refugees by the Home Office. This chapter reflects how the pandemic exacerbated many of the problems which were experienced by asylum seekers and refugees during the pandemic and how they were compounded alongside new barriers to identification and support. Highlighting the other issues and challenges they faced once the restrictions from the pandemic were lifted is an important and often overlooked issue which requires attention. Specifically, these were the length of time asylum seekers had to wait for their decisions from the Home Office and secondly, the ongoing housing crisis which affects the provision of accommodation being given to asylum seekers as a priority need and at the expense of UK nationals. The chapter states how the increased number of backlogged asylum cases are being processed by the Home Office and the pressure which is felt by local authorities to house asylum seekers is contributing to a deterioration in their mental health. It discusses the role the organisation played in supporting asylum seekers and refugees given the hostile treatment by some sections of the media, political establishment and parts of the electorate.

**Keywords** Asylum Seekers · Refugees · Covid-19 · Pandemic

43

M. Davis, *Third Sector Organisations, Asylum Seekers and Refugees*, https://doi.org/10.1007/978-3-031-85137-7_6

Today, the two main challenges asylum seekers and refugees are exposed to post-pandemic are 1) the length of time to wait for asylum decisions from the Home Office due to the asylum cases backlog, and 2) the ongoing housing crisis in the UK which makes the provision of accommodation from the government to foreign nationals politically and socially challenging:

> Things like the cost-of-living crisis that affect all of us in the UK, we often get the sharp end of it with who we support. Crisis regards legal aid, lots of people we support do not have lawyers and we cannot get them lawyers. So that's been really difficult. Similarly, like the housing crisis now with people getting refugee status, there is a general housing crisis and then the people who get the worst of that are the most vulnerable.[1]

In 2023, 84,425 people applied for asylum in the UK.[2] As discussed in the last section, waiting for decisions from the Home Office is a significant issue for asylum seekers. There are delays to processing asylum claims by the Home Office due to lower numbers of caseworkers and the complexities of claims which make decisions longer. Available statistics show the number of people waiting for an initial decision increased from 70,000 in 2020 to 166,300 in 2022 with 68% of those waiting more than six months and 32% waiting less than six months or less.[3] As of June 2023, 138,000 cases were awaiting an initial decision.[4] As of December 2023, there were 95,000 cases without an initial decision.[5] A consequence of delays to asylum seekers receiving decisions is the risk of them going missing and falling into the black economy and at risk of being exploited.

[1] Participant B1.

[2] Georgina Sturge, "Asylum statistics," House of Commons Library, 1 March 2024 at 5.

[3] Joe Tyler-Todd, Georgina Sturge and CJ McKinney, "Delays to processing asylum claims in the UK," Research Briefing Number CBP 9737, 20 March 2023.

[4] Georgina Sturge, "Asylum statistics," House of Commons Library, 1 March 2024 at 5.

[5] Georgina Sturge, "Asylum statistics," House of Commons Library, 1 March 2024 at 5.

The Home Office recently admitted that up to 17,000 asylum seekers are missing and are unaccounted for.[6]

The issue regarding the lack of legal representation has already been highlighted. However, in cases where some asylum seekers have a support worker involved, the language barrier is a significant issue where explanations and communication of decisions and the effect of the decision letters is difficult for them to understand. Alongside the language barrier, the fact that many people are in an unfamiliar country is challenging because of cultural differences:

> There are lots of cultural differences in the UK with getting used to life here, especially if someone has not been in the UK too long, I know how it can be a big adjustment for some and help and assistance is required.[7]

Many asylum seekers and refugees require help with practical tasks such as registering for services and accessing public transport. Whilst some of these tasks are the same for all asylum seekers and refugees, it has been acknowledged that the challenges for some asylum seekers are very diverse to others. Different groups of asylum seekers have their own individual diverse challenges which are highlighted and described below:

> Every and each group has their own struggles, I would say that there's some things that are the same for everyone, then some particular struggles for families. But then single male asylum seekers have some other challenges too.[8]

Whilst asylum seekers are waiting for decisions to arrive from the Home Office there are lots of feelings of isolation and being left in limbo as when decisions do not arrive in a timely manner there are feelings of anxiety and about what their future looks like. This has a big impact on mental health. Asylum seekers require a sense of security which the system with its delays currently does not provide certainty especially where asylum seekers are having to wait many months for their decisions.

---

[6] Rajeev Syal, "Home Office 'loses' 17,000 people whose asylum claims were withdrawn," The Guardian, 29 November 2023, accessed at https://www.theguardian.com/world/2023/nov/29/home-office-loses-17000-asylum-seekers-registered-in-britain.

[7] Participant B2.

[8] Participant B5.

There is also a huge difficulty in accessing NHS services due to how over-whelmed services are for UK citizens with significant waits for referrals, appointments, treatments, procedures, scans and operations.[9]

The issue of homelessness becomes a more significant one after people get 'Leave to Remain' in the UK. Staff explained that the pressure to accommodate families is not as great as the local authority housing single men. Essentially, local authorities do not consider single men priority need, and so will only offer emergency accommodation to families with children under 18, and so single men (and women) often become home-less. Whilst someone's claim is being processed, most people are entitled to Sect. 95 support. However, the consequences are that single men tend to be stigmatised, impacting their mental health. It has been found from the research that men are struggling for a variety of reasons including the inability to access mental health support, and because there is a social stigma attached to this group, identifying them as economic migrants, and not genuine asylum seekers:

> There is a stereotypical approach to single young men as if they are here just to work. This obviously isn't the case. Obviously, there are economic migrants but having an asylum process in place is not about whether a single person is here to work or not, it is about torture, it is about abuse, it is about exploitation in some ways too.[10]

As many asylum seekers have travelled long distances to reach the UK, the mental health of people who AX help seems to be a big issue which requires attention because of the trauma many asylum seekers have been through alongside embarking on treacherous journeys:

> Mental health is a big and emerging issue that seems to be more present in the people we help. I know that it is a very big issue for teams in the UK. By the time we are available to help them they have already been through some horrendous and traumatising events, not just from the country they

---

[9] British Medical Association, "NHS backlog data analysis," 15 March 2024, accessed at https://www.bma.org.uk/advice-and-support/nhs-delivery-and-workforce/pressures/nhs-backlog-data-analysis#:~:text=around%203.5%20million%20of%20these,December%202023%20figure%20of%20337%2C000.

[10] Participant B1.

have left but also from the journey as well. We meet a lot of people who I can see even with an untrained eye are carrying a lot of trauma.[11]

As previously highlighted, refugees are experiencing a new set of challenges to when they were asylum seekers. It is almost the end of having to navigate one set of services and then when they become refugees, they are exposed to finding their way through difficulties associated with having to navigate their way through a new set of issues and barriers. When asylum seekers gain refugee status the main priority is for them to access accommodation. This is challenging because of the existing social problem with UK citizens accessing permanent social housing, rather than navigating through the temporary accommodation sector. When asylum seekers become refugees, they have 28 days to find accommodation before their services and support stop.[12] This is a difficult situation for refugees to find themselves in:

> Lots of people are getting their claims accepted now and getting refugee status and then needing to access the whole system of setting up their life permanently in the UK and this has been very challenging for a lot of people. There's a lot of people being made homeless because they just cannot find housing in time.[13]

A further problem is that AX do not work with asylum seekers after they have received refugee status and therefore, this is an issue for refugees knowing where else they can go to access support:

> We do not work with them once they have status, so that is something we've been looking at now and how does that change now that this is the bigger problem. The bigger problem now is that people are becoming homeless.[14]

Even in situations where refugees receive accommodation the standard of the housing can often be very poor:

[11] Participant B3.

[12] Kwame Boakye, "Refugees facing 'life on the streets' without change to Home Office housing rules," Local Government Chronicle, 15 January 2024.

[13] Participant B1.

[14] Participant B6.

We have had situations where there were people living with children and there were rats which was not taken seriously by authorities. We had to strongly advocate for those families.[15]

Consequently, many refugees feel disappointment when they are in the UK as the perception of how things would be is very different to what they imagined:

There's almost this kind of relief of we've made it to this destination that we really hold in high esteem, and we think this is where we are going to be safe, and we are going to be treated fairly and somewhere we can start our lives again.[16]

Therefore, staff and volunteers have been trained to manage the expectations of asylum seekers and refugees, explaining that how they may see things may not be what the reality is. Back in Europe where AX is continuing their work, a significant issue is how climate change is affecting their work. Firstly, a big issue is the weather with "floods common with many houses, villages and small communities that are underwater at the moment."[17] Consequently, AX have had to adapt to support people:

The clothes people are wearing are the only clothes they have, and they are not waterproof. We have been really focussed on waterproof clothing the last few weeks, we have given out nearly 1,000 items of waterproof clothing and it is not enough.[18]

As highlighted in the introduction, AX work in a tempestuous environment which is hostile to immigrants from some quarters of society within the European location in which they are based. The politicalisation of immigration feeds into a negative rhetoric against asylum seekers and refugees through policy and language aimed at deterring asylum seekers and not making them feel welcome. This is evidenced from testimony from one staff member who works in the European operation about riot

---

[15] Participant B5.
[16] Participant B3.
[17] Participant B3.
[18] Participant B3.

police who states that the surveillance from the police towards asylum seekers tends to have increased:

> There has been lots of tv coverage with water cannons being used against protestors, those same people come here to monitor the refugee situation. They conduct four hourly evictions of living sites here so every 14 hours they go into a living site and take the sleeping bags.

This constant surveillance appears to be something which is growing stronger since the pandemic where "constant harassment and moving on is common, forcing more people to live in smaller and smaller confined spaces to try and hide from the police."[19] For one staff member, it is very horrible to witness and is reported to be the worst it has ever been since working for AX.

---

[19] Participant B3.

# CHAPTER 7

# Reflections of the Work of AX by Staff Members to Address the Challenges of Asylum Seekers and Refugees

**Abstract** This chapter reflects how staff evaluated their performance in assisting and supporting during the pandemic and what lessons can be learnt during this period. It is important to illustrate this because it directs where best practice can be observed for future pandemics alongside improving new ways of meeting the issues faced by asylum seekers and refugees. This chapter examines how the present challenges which asylum seekers and refugees are subjected to should now be addressed by the organisation as it moves forward into the future. The question which is asked here is what issues need to be addressed to meet the aims and objectives for asylum seekers and refugees, namely given the impact on the staff and volunteers' mental health within the organisation. The purpose of this chapter is to evaluate some of the concerns staff have which directly impact their work on the frontline. It looks at some of the policies and procedures within the organisation to consider whether some of them need to be amended given the experience of working within a pandemic. The chapter demonstrates the many positive traits the organisation displays but also signals some of the legitimate concerns some staff have regarding the outside political and social resentment towards refugees generally.

**Keywords** Asylum Seekers · Refugees · Covid-19 · Pandemic

© The Author(s), under exclusive license to Springer Nature Switzerland AG 2025
M. Davis, *Third Sector Organisations, Asylum Seekers and Refugees*,
https://doi.org/10.1007/978-3-031-85137-7_7

51

The previous section examined the challenges asylum seekers face whilst being supported and assisted by AX post-pandemic. A question which will now be raised is how effectively the organisation is meeting the challenges which asylum seekers find themselves in? To answer this question, the research examines the views of staff to understand the positive aspects of the organisation and what issues need to be addressed to meet the aims and objectives for asylum seekers and refugees alongside looking at the health and welfare of employees and volunteers as part of their work and support. The tone of this report changes to becoming reflective by reporting the positive aspects of AX's work directly from the frontline staff. The purpose of this section is to evaluate some of the issues staff have within their work which directly enhance or conversely impact their ability to help and support asylum seekers and refugees. The following section also explains the concerns some staff have which directly impact their work on the frontline assisting and supporting asylum seekers and refugees.

As already acknowledged, a significant contribution is made by staff and volunteers to the needs of asylum seekers and refugees. Many employees within the organisation possess a wide range of previous experience with other charities before working there with some having experience of supporting asylum seekers alongside other vulnerable groups, primarily in support worker roles. It has been shown to be a very collaborative organisation between staff and volunteers. Staff are extremely thankful for the work the core group of reliable volunteers do and have a lot of admiration for them because of the dedication, and commitment they show towards the cause, alongside the empathy they show for the people they support:

> I think that the volunteers are incredibly supportive of the cause and aims. We have some long-time volunteers who have been here for a few years. I think the amazing thing is how much our volunteers are willing to do and how much expertise they have.[1]

Interestingly, AX possess some volunteers who have lived experiences of being an asylum seeker and now a refugee. This enhances the diversity of the organisation because of the connection of someone being a service user to working in AX to continue support:

[1] Participant B1.

So, they have been previous service users and I really love that because you cannot have a better service that when it is service led. When an organisation has people with some life experience, we have real voices heard from the ground and I am really proud that we have people like that helping us and others.[2]

Staff members are extremely proud to be working in an organisation which has a fantastic cause associated with it. Despite the harassment and trolling on social media threatening violence and attention from far-right groups who attend hotels where asylum seekers and refugees are being temporarily accommodated which does occasionally happen, staff and volunteers remain undeterred in continuing the support and help provided to asylum seekers and refugees. This is testament to there being an abundance of respect towards the asylum seeker and refugee community within the organisation which continues to provide a clear and empowering objective of AX:

The most important thing that we can do is to respect the communities that we are working with and ensure that we get much needed items to the people who need it, in the safest possible way.[3]

Part of the work is about staff and volunteers being vocal about the issues and policies which directly impact the lives of asylum seekers and refugees. The recognition from the people they help is a significant benefit for staff and volunteers to be involved with the organisation and indeed other similar charities who help and support refugees. One such example of other similar charities advocating for refugees was the calling out a policy which had a detrimental impact on asylum seekers is the policy of accommodating asylum seekers on the Bibby Stockholm vessel,[4] where a legal challenge was brought by lawyers against the use of accommodation for asylum seekers. AX stepped back from this legal challenge. Consequently, there is a strong sense of pride which comes with being associated with the organisation which is reflected by staff:

[2] Participant B7.

[3] Participant B3.

[4] Melanie Gower, "Asylum accommodation: hotels, vessels and large-scale sites," House of Commons Library, Research Briefing, 7 July 2023, accessed at https://researchbriefings.files.parliament.uk/documents/CBP-9831/CBP-9831.pdf.

I'm really proud of the organisation. I like how outspoken we are, and it often feels like we are addressing a need that other groups do not do.[5]

AX continue to have a strong advocacy presence, matched with lots of positive energy and momentum which is being pushed along by staff and volunteers on an energetic platform to represent and be a strong voice of activism:

> It's really good for us to advocate for their rights and equip volunteers to advocate for refugees as it is really important. It is a really big part of what we do. Change will not come from our politicians, it will come from grassroots organisations.[6]

It is difficult for some staff members to see the efforts of their work from an organisational perspective as statistic information in the European operation is kept at a very low minimum and lack of emphasis regards General Data Protection Regulations (GDPR):

> We do not collect any official statistics...we do not register anyone or collects any stats as where we work it is a very transient place. The basis of what we do is humanitarian support so the documentation and recording of people is not something we do. We do not have the expertise to do that work safely, our work is to fill in the gaps of support which is not provided by the State.[7]

Having said that the organisation does employ a dedicated expert person who deals with this issue alongside producing Quality Assurance Data. Statistics and data are collated and useful to identify new and existing areas of support which can be funded in the future, so data is really important to make this a reality to strengthen the assistance offered and provided to asylum seekers and refugees. AX is an influential organisation, one which operates in a difficult working environment where the politicisation of migrants and refugees operates in a hostile and aggressive narrative when topics of immigration are discussed. Nevertheless, AX exists as a significant voice which is demonstrated by staff:

[5] Participant B1.

[6] Participant B3.

[7] Participant B3.

I think since 2015/2016 we have grown into an effective organisation. We are unique as we have both a UK and European perspective where we can join up our services and work closely together. In terms of care and its operations I hope other people say we are an effective operation.[8]

Staff believe one of the reasons why there are an effective organisation is the ability to adapt their support for asylum seekers and refugees in response to government policies. One staff member was able to clearly articulate how AX quickly responds to the needs of asylum seekers:

Every time the government comes out with a new policy, we work out how it affects the people we help and how we can support them. I think it comes down to the energy within the organisation, and the feeling of wanting to address the biggest need.[9]

For the organisation to effectively function as it does, there needs to be a loose structure in place and autonomy with AX is present which allows to run things differently and change how they operate which has both benefits and drawbacks:

The individual local groups can respond quickly without having to check things through a big chain of command with many rules and procedures to follow. We are rather fluid in that way which is not always a good thing. There are downsides to that. But it does make us adaptable.[10]

Flexibility and autonomy of staff is a present theme within the staff which is judged to be a good thing and something which continues to be constant. It shows how empowered staff can be to make a big impact on their own roles, evidenced by the following statement:

I actually really like the fact that we are given such a huge amount in terms of the management of how we work and the decision-making process and stuff.[11]

---

[8] Participant B3.

[9] Participant B1.

[10] Participant B1.

[11] Participant B7.

One benefit to working remotely was the fact that it is a very flexible job where the work can be done in many parts of the UK. This is very appealing to some staff as they do not need to be tied to a specific location to fulfil their job responsibilities. It was something which one staff member had to adjust to during the Covid-19 pandemic. Nevertheless, the team helped the staff member overcome any barriers:

> I had spent Covid-19 working for another company we went through a period of transforming into my role being remote. It changed the way I approached my work and I found that when I joined here, I actually liked it.[12]

In terms of organisational structure, it was reported that staff believe that there is a clear chain of command with different responsibility roles attached to the organisation. However, this does not mean to say that the organisation operates as a vertical structure, i.e. a top-down hierarchical organisation. In fact, the reverse appears to be the case. It shows that it operates as a horizontal chain of command, with many different teams working on different things and then they all feed in together. Consequently, it is easy for staff to move around teams in a relatively straightforward manner:

> As the charity continues to expand, the need for new roles to be created will grow as well as people having to move around and take on other tasks and responsibilities which is continuing happening.[13]

AX is working through a period of transition which involves restructuring and developing new policies and procedures for staff and volunteers. This change is something that has been welcomed by many staff and has been asked for a long time to take place.[14] Additionally, a new CEO was announced which meant that there before this it was an unsettling time, "with a huge amount of turbulence and confusion as to what it is that we are actually doing and how are we going to do it."[15] Hopefully,

[12] Participant B7.
[13] Participant B2.
[14] Participant B5.
[15] Participant B6.

the arrival of the new CEO reduces the previous turbulence and confusion by addressing structures, policies and procedures going forward. As staff have been asking for more structure to be constructed within the organisation, one participant was pleased to see how this has started to take place and has benefits of reducing the risk of burnout amongst staff and volunteers. The new appointment signalled a fresh start and positive changes in the structure of the organisation as highlighted by one staff member:

> Before the new CEO came onboard, I did not know what other departments existed, but now we are slowly getting there where we have more meetings together and starting to work together.[16]

In addition, support for staff and volunteers through increased training has been introduced. These have focussed on assisting staff and volunteers to maintain self-care as the work with asylum seekers and refugees can often lead to burnout and fatigue. There are courses and sessions on suicide prevention, grounding, bereavement, sleep and psychosis which have been introduced by other staff members and in some cases volunteer-led:

> We have biweekly meetings where people can share their struggles, it's not therapy as such, but it's a therapeutic group run initiative for volunteers, by volunteers.[17]

However, the events are not often well attended because of workload pressures, preventing more staff and volunteers being able to effectively contribute to the sessions. The type of sessions are questions at present with the need for wellbeing supervision of staff and volunteers taking place in a therapeutic environment on a group and/or individual basis:

> It is stipulated for certain professions that it is legally required for clinical supervision and that basically means counselling. It means there must be space for counselling and although it is not in our rules, it is evidence of good practice.[18]

---

[16] Participant B6.
[17] Participant B5.
[18] Participant B7.

This reflective practice initiative would be most useful and practical in the circumstances, as it was acknowledged that "it would really support people, giving a private space to share things within a group and to have access to some really important resources and be equipped with the knowledge and tools they may need to help them."[19] A confidant, someone who is impartial to speak with is also raised as a possibility.[20] The issue of cost of providing this support and training was raised at this point. AX do not have the funds to provide such substantial support. However, the need for such sessions not only shows how useful they can be to staff and volunteers but also because without them there is a risk of exacerbating the problem of not retaining volunteers and them leaving the organisation. Retention of staff and volunteers appears to be a problem within the organisation. This is not necessarily specific to AX, but to all charities and organisations with unpaid volunteers who give up their own time to a cause. Volunteer retention is a problem, but AX acknowledges the difficulty of knowing what additional support is required:

> Generally, I do think we have a problem with volunteer retention. People become signed up and have the induction training and then they do not quite know where they fit in or just get sort of burnt out. It's something we are thinking about, how do we improve the rates of volunteer retention? So, I think it is providing more support for them, but often it is difficult to work out what support is best.[21]

There are many financial pressures associated with running an organisation. They exist within a tension of demand for services from service users balanced with the resources of an organisation. Despite such a large operation which the organisation undertakes, AX has no fundraising team to generate more income. However, they do have fundraising in other ways, through a communications teams through supporters. As part of defining specific roles for specific volunteers, one participant expressed how important it is to maximise the skills of volunteers in their level of expertise:

---

[19] Participant B2.
[20] Participant B7.
[21] Participant B1.

I think having its own fundraising department is so important. Something I have wanted to work on is defining specific roles for volunteers so that we have a different skill set within different roles, so it is not just volunteering as such, it is being very focussed on one specific type of assistance.[22]

Earlier in the section it highlighted the issue of low attendance of wellbeing classes due to workload pressures and a lack of time to attend sessions. The issue of long hours and excessive workloads is a significant issue across most areas in businesses and organisations. There is often a strong demand for services but the availability of labour to satisfy the demand falls behind. As the new CEO arrived the issue of the huge demand to help asylum seekers and refugees was fed into the initial concerns from staff with the view that the organisation requires many more paid positions so that a bigger staff team will be able to handle the existing workload:

> We had a new CEO and he's been really good at trying to create a positive culture. I think the only issue that really comes up is the capacity issue. We are such a small team doing quite a lot of work across the country and I think there are times where we often feel unsupported. We work long hours because we work with volunteers and a lot of the work we do is outside hours, in the evenings and weekends. And that can be very stressful.[23]

Easing capacity so that staff can have some pressure taken off them would be beneficial. Staff expressed concern that there are no meetings with management to discuss operational and wellbeing issues as well as no present opportunity to facilitate a dialogue with Trustees to voice their concerns to and the desire to have more support from management to address recurrent issues associated with their work:

> We do need better training for senior management level in terms of their responsibilities as managers, not just to manage the presenting fires that they are putting out...because that is what they are doing, firefighting. You know things like bereavement leave, people with additional responsibilities, any protected characteristics are completely forgotten about.[24]

[22] Participant B6.

[23] Participant B1.

[24] Participant B7.

Visibility of trustees is an issue which a staff member would appreciate being addressed along with having the opportunity to discuss their work with them and for staff and volunteers to know more about Trustees and the skills they bring to the organisation:

> The main thing is for the Trustees wo be visible by the staff team. We need to know more about them, what their skill sets are and understand when it is ok for us to go to them to use their specialist skill for something. I would love for Trustees to be approachable. Also, each member of staff could be given the opportunity on a rota basis to go to the Board meetings to find out what is going on and to voice our concerns.[25]

Also, more specific knowledge at the senior level is required to be had which was a concern of one staff member:

> We all need to be trained. Senior management did not know that there are many different types of abuse or what they looked like. I would like everyone to be trained at the minimum of Level 2 safeguarding.[26]

The concern is that staff and volunteers find it hard to psychologically switch off from the work they are undertaking and the emotional support they are providing to asylum seekers and refugees. Staff are increasingly concerned about this:

> I think the tricky thing is that with this line of work, they often do not turn off, right? So, making sure boundaries are really important.[27]

The organisation ensuring a work/life balance for staff has been highlighted as a problem. Many staff report that they are working long hours which is impacting their health:

> The amount of work and how it impacts on my work/life balance is not something I am comfortable with and I have been quite vocal about this since I joined. I am afraid to say that I do not have a life outside of AX. Every week I am roughly doing 60-70 hours without fail. I am tired and not sleeping and eating and making me make mistakes. I do not wish to

---

[25] Participant B7.

[26] Participant B7.

[27] Participant B6.

make out that I am a perfectionist but the mistakes I made are not mistakes I would normally make.[28]

Additionally, one staff member reported how overwhelmed it made the staff member feel after the weekend where there was a huge number of messages on the phone which needed to be responded to, leading to their mental health being impacted:

> Probably on a Friday evening, about half 8 – 9pm I would turn it off and then on Monday morning at 8.30am I wait to see that the average number of 50 Whatsapp messages and it just makes you feel sick.[29]

To combat the anxiety, one staff member resorted to installing their own work boundaries from their private life due to the fact that the staff member was using their own phone for work calls which was unhealthy and made them think whether removing themselves from the organisation is a viable action in order to take to preserve their physical and mental health:

> Because the lack of boundaries that were in place I ended up buying myself a work phone because I could not sperate my private life with friends and family from my work life and so my phone was giving me anxiety. I needed to maybe step back from my role now because my health and well-being is my priority.

As discussed in the previous section, AX has the advantage of having well experienced staff and volunteers who have supported asylum seekers, refugees and individuals from other social groups through various organisations. However, the concern from some staff is the reluctance of not overwhelming volunteers with work and this remains a concern. Staff are concerned about volunteers completing onerous tasks which may distract them from doing the volunteer work they originally joined the organisation to do:

> You are constantly putting in policies and procedures and asking them to fill out forms, making sure that they are doing their risk assessments,

---

[28] Participant B7.

[29] Participant B7.

making sure that they are being accountable to what we are doing for service users.[30]

Due to the issues highlighted above, burnout of staff and volunteers is a significant risk. Again, this is in no way specific to this organisation.[31] However, burnout remains a real risk to higher numbers of volunteers leaving. Vicarious trauma, burnout and the impact on the retention of staff is a significant issue in frontline organisations, including the anti-slavery sector.[32] Consequently, the effect of burnout has been seen with a desire for more emphasis being placed on self-care:

> I have seen someone in the organisation who was exhausted from everything we are doing. I think there has been a cultural shift with the new CEO. I think we need to look after ourselves a bit more and have better boundaries in place with a culture of self-care.[33]

An idea is to contact past volunteers and reaching out to them to understand the reasons more clearly why they left AX and what else could have been done to retain their voluntary services. It is acknowledged that "it would be so useful to find out and get feedback why they left so we can improve things in the future."[34] Culture was a word which came through the words of staff during some of the interviews. The new CEO has instilled a new working culture and staff believe that staff are more open about what they are experiencing when helping and supporting asylum seekers and refugees and how the work is making them feel:

> When volunteers must deal with someone who is suicidal that is very upsetting. I think we are better at practising a culture where they can share this

---

[30] Participant B6.

[31] See Jack Larkham and Mariam Mansoor, "Running hot, burning out," Pro Bono Economics Nottingham Trent University, March 2023, accessed at https://www.probon oeconomics.com/Handlers/Download.ashx?IDMF=469023 1e-ae66-4fbe-8a4e-9d51e1 6ed187.

[32] "Vicarious Trauma, Burnout and Staff Retention in the Anti-Slavery Sector," Human Trafficking Foundation, August 2023, accessed at https://static1.squarespace. com/static/599abfb4e6f2e19ff048494f/t/64d3b77aad96c75413e09c22/169159666 6470/HTF+Post+Event+Briefing.pdf.

[33] Participant B1.

[34] Participant B2.

experience and talk about it as an issue which they need help with. In the past volunteers have often felt alone because they did not have that direct communication to ask someone for help. It must have felt an isolating experience.[35]

However, there is a perceived culture from one staff member who believes that this is something which still needs to be worked on:

It seems from what I have been told that the culture was they (staff) are concerned to voice things and would be spoken down to and treated badly. There is also a culture of you are never off duty.[36]

This section has identified and examined different aspects of AX's work from an employee perspective. They illustrate the many positive traits that the organisations show and how staff contribute by using their own experience, skills and knowledge to help and support asylum seekers and refugees. They also highlight some of the concerns staff have which are consequences to engaging with this type of frontline work and the challenges they face. Considering this the next section examines what the significant present challenges for AX are which can be addressed and actioned to continue the existing work and enhance the aims and objectives of AX with an enthusiastic, committed, conscientious, motivated and empathetic workforce.

[35] Participant B1.
[36] Participant B7.

# CHAPTER 8

# The Significant Challenges for Organisation AX Moving Forward

**Abstract** This chapter specifically looks through the lens of the organisation to establish what it can identify as the main challenges for the organisation going forward post-pandemic as they continue their work with refugees. This part of the research examines the main issues for the organisation based on the research findings above, and respectfully offers recommendations. It outlines some of the main issues which are being focussed upon by the organisation alongside considering the opportunities for the organisation to move forward and adapt to the specific needs of this vulnerable and marginalised group within society.

**Keywords** Asylum Seekers · Refugees · Charities

Considering the challenges experienced by staff and volunteers during and after the pandemic, it is worth reflecting on that time by understanding what the main challenges for AX will be as they move forward to continuing their support and assistance to asylum seekers and refugees in a post-pandemic environment.

This section of the research will identify and examine the main issues for the organisation are based on the findings concerning the challenges asylum seekers and refugees encounter post-pandemic alongside the views from staff in the previous section. They are discussed in no order, or

© The Author(s), under exclusive license to Springer Nature
Switzerland AG 2025
M. Davis, *Third Sector Organisations, Asylum Seekers and Refugees*,
https://doi.org/10.1007/978-3-031-85137-7_8

priority. The purpose of this section is to bring out what can be improved within the organisation to form recommendations for AX to adopt and implement.

The organisation continues to be a significant voice in the advocacy of rights of asylum seekers and refugees. This is clearly seen from the interviews with staff which took place. Although AX has been through a very disruptive period to its leadership, the impression given is that the organisation is progressing forward, despite many challenges:

> "We're moving forward now. I've started my role with a clean slate and having that flexibility to make it my own things and work with others has been beneficial. We have moved on from the turbulence and are moving into a new period but are not quite sure what it looks like yet."[1]

As discussed in the last section, a new CEO has been appointed within AX by trustees. Therefore, it will take time for any new culture which is set to be embedded within AX to take shape. So far, the responses to the new CEO have been largely positive. One of the biggest challenges for AX appears to be the demand of services and support from asylum seekers and refugees alongside the capacity issue to provide these resources from staff and volunteers from AX:

> "We cannot reach demand; we have to make such horrendously difficult decisions about distributions about who we say yes to and who we do not."[2]

Whilst AX is not in control of the movement of migrants and asylum seekers and the policies implemented to combat the flow of asylum seekers, AX has a challenge of being able to recruit new staff albeit if finances allow and to retain existing staff and volunteers. It is suggested that not having additional staff reduces the effectiveness of the organisation to help those who rely on them for support:

> We are going to have an army of asylum seekers who will fall through the gaps through no fault of their own, but we are doing them an injustice

---

[1] Participant B6.

[2] Participant B3.

right now by not having the resources to make a better and bigger staff team and to have clearer boundaries, clear rules and guidance.[3]

AX work in a hostile political environment to asylum seekers and refugees. They are not policymakers but adjust their ways of working to help people despite the legislative measures and policies by governments:

> It's a revolving door of setting up something one minute, and then having to change it because the government decides they're going to do something else or bring in a new policy. Part of our work is about keeping up with the changes that are happening as they constantly change. Our work will never be done.[4]

Whilst they continue to challenge specific policies such as the Rwanda policy and the use of Bibby Stockholm for example, they are always on guard to consider and make swift changes to their work to meet the needs of asylum seekers and refugees in a humanitarian way. Often, AX deal with the human fallout and consequences of such policies of government.

The organisation has seen more instances of harassment of volunteers and the detainment of staff by authorities in Europe which may serve as a deterrent for new staff and volunteers to work for AX and for existing staff to continue being so vocal towards the policies against asylum seekers:

> The police have started to detain British nationals working as humanitarian aid workers here, they have started to enforce passport rules, visa rules. They detained two British nationals for not carrying their passports with them, even though it's not a legal requirement. And they were detained for 23 hours even though after two hours of that detention they provided their passports.[5]

An issue which seems to be growing is the level of paperwork involved which is required to be completed by staff. As this side of the organisation needs to be fulfilled, staff did say that it can often be distracting them from the real work to be done. One suggestion to address this is as follows:

[3] Participant B7.

[4] Participant B6.

[5] Participant B3.

Maybe it is time to have more part time staff members who can help with the paperwork side of things and be present in these moments. It is then their paid role to get that stuff done which is what we need in the organisation.[6]

What may be useful is the introduction of a staff handbook and a volunteer handbook. Staff could include what they believe are the main ways of solving issues within the organisation and is a resource for all staff to consult when required. Likewise, a volunteer handbook could set out the rights and expectation of volunteers in a codified manner. A flowchart of assistance could be incorporated into the handbooks for clarity as advocated by a staff member:

> We could have a picture on our website as to what he journey when you come through AX for assistance will look like and what you can expect to receive in terms of direct aid, how often you can expect it and how we will assist with moving service users on when they get refugee status.[7]

Combined with this, there is a need for a Human Resources partner to be brought onboard and visible to staff and volunteers who could facilitate the above alongside managing reasonable adjustments needed by staff and occupational health assessments. At present, it is said that there is one person who looks after annual leave requests and tracks holidays.[8] Staff and volunteer appraisals could also take place through this new partner.

One issue is the continued provision of humanitarian aid and being able to deliver and provide such aid to those who need it. Due to the cost-of-living crisis, costs for fuel and food have substantially increased and AX have found that the donations which they receive are not stretching as far as what they used to. As a consequence of Brexit, it is not commercially viable to import food from the UK as that used to be the cheapest option for them. In addition, they are finding that the levels of donations have reduced too:

[6] Participant B6.

[7] Participant B7.

[8] Participant B7.

We are seeing a real decrease in the number of donations we receive and in terms of clothing. That was the real backbone of all our operations.[9]

AX helps and support many different types of asylum seekers and refugees. One specific group identified in the research was single men. Therefore, as the numbers of single men who come into contact with AX, it would be reasonable to understand what if any additional support needs are required to support them and whether AX are able to facilitate this support, especially after they receive a positive asylum decision from the Home Office. It was highlighted earlier in the research how single men have less access to mental health support and are not classed as having priority needs. It is seen that local authorities can accommodate families more easily than single men and will be a challenge for AX to support going forward. Furthermore, focussing on reducing the stigma, stereotypical attitudes and fighting against discrimination against single men asylum seekers who face challenges accessing mental health support should be advocated. Alongside this will be understanding and accepting what are the responsibilities of AX to assisting asylum seekers who then become refugees if they become homeless because of a lack of accommodation. The present situation lends itself to the Home Office reducing the asylum backlog and therefore making more decisions. This places pressure on the accommodation of refugees. AX may wish to think about its role it sees itself playing to continuing the support to refugees who they helped as asylum seekers and whether the emphasis will be more on supporting refugees rather than asylum seekers:

> We do not work with people who have recently received their status as refugees, so this is something we have been looking at now and how does that change the organisation. The bigger problem now is that people are becoming homeless.[10]

It may be a difficult balance to provide support to both groups given the pressures of allocating resources. As the research identifies there are more refugees being made homeless due to difficulties accessing housing. A question for AX would look something like, "what are the obligations of the organisation to refugees due to the impact of homelessness on this

---

[9] Participant B3.
[10] Participant B6.

social group?" A broader question would be "what duties and responsibilities do they have to refugees now that they have the right to stay in the UK?" This is really important as answering this question will set out the vision of AX going forward into the future. Understanding what the organisation can do as well as what the organisation cannot do is crucial:

> One of the challenges is that making sure we stay in our lane and that everyone knows what it is that AX do because it's so easy to try and do a bit of everything and then find out that you are helping no-one.[11]

The way in which AX protects staff is also an important challenge which was highlighted by some staff. There is a perception that "they are not aware of their duties as employers to look after the wellbeing of their staff."[12] Consequently, this may be a barrier for some staff to step back from their role to focus on their health which is a priority. There is no question how committed staff are in maintaining the wellbeing of volunteers, but this also can come at the cost of the health of staff:

> The irony is that I am leading a group of volunteers whilst I am taking medication prescribed by my GP because of the impact that this type of work is having on me is ridiculous.[13]

Therefore, reasonable adjustments of staff would be useful to be documented and recorded by Human Resources and for a chain of command to be made aware of any personal issues which may affect their work and work around them. The retention of volunteers has already been cited as a challenge for AX. Additionally, there is a need for AX to recruit new volunteers into AX. There may be barriers for some people who wish to volunteer but are not able to access online communications such as Zoom or MS Teams because of digital poverty. Alternatively, they may not have the technological skills to navigate their way around the systems AX use:

> There is a level of need for people to access Zoom which some volunteers simply cannot do. We do have one volunteer who is 90 years old, she isn't going to be able to get onto Zoom to access training etc. So, we have

---

[11] Participant B6.

[12] Participant B7.

[13] Participant B7.

a personal volunteer who goes to help her access this stuff and does the meetings with her as she doesn't have access because she doesn't have a computer.[14]

The training of staff in specific areas may be something which AX wishes to look at. Staff reported that as part of their work they did not see any instances of human smuggling or human trafficking taking place when working. Increased awareness of what modern slavery, human trafficking and human smuggling looks like may be issues which staff and particularly volunteers wish to undertake so that they will be able to spot the signs of this behaviour and act upon concerns. To counter the issue that there is a gap in knowledge on the various types of abuse, the whole organisation could be trained by an external provider as evidence of CPD engagement.

Due to the type of work involved on the frontline, the ways and methods of how AX continues to support staff will be crucial to keep well-being and retention of staff and volunteers. For example, support towards staff installing suitable boundaries so that they are able to switch off after work due to the exposure of listening and engaging with people of trauma and having negative past experiences:

> I think it can definitely take its toll on people who are working in this sector because inherently people do it because they care.[15]

It was advocated that it is important to "establish good boundaries to show how you are looking after your own well-being."[16] The suggestion has been made for the organisation to know what the boundaries to their work are and then for each staff and volunteer to adopt their own boundaries to meet the aims and objectives of the organisation. Staff and volunteers should be able to effectively communicate them to each other in a way which will be respected by management. There is a suggestion that the organisation says 'yes' too often and the management either do not understand or are blind to the emotional, physical and psychological impacts of the work undertaken.[17]

---

[14] Participant B6.

[15] Participant B2.

[16] Participant B7.

[17] Participant B7.

As volunteers play an important and significant role in the organisation and because they are often exposed to traumatised asylum seekers and refugees, they are tasked with having to provide a lot of emotional support. The pressures placed on volunteers can often be overwhelming and a reason why volunteers can often leave the organisation impacting on retention rates of volunteers:

> We've got some amazing volunteers that do it, but we've also got a lot of volunteers who have left or stepped down from doing as much because they say it's just too much.[18]

The impact of listening to peoples' trauma on volunteers is something which should not be underestimated:

> There's a lot of things going on with the people that we work with, they have trauma. And trauma likes to hide. And then in a way, it's transferred onto volunteers.[19]

Often there are safeguarding issues involved, especially if they are suicidal. It is often very difficult for volunteers and staff to hear such terrible stories because the transference of trauma takes place often. Likewise, it can be very challenging for staff and volunteers to be exposed to the daily struggles asylum seekers and refugees have. It is normal for volunteers and staff to take on this emotion and take it home with them once they finish work or volunteering. An issue is how does the organisation internally respond to the needs of staff and volunteers in these cases. A challenge for AX is establishing a comprehensive and financially supported approach to guaranteeing the correct professional supervision either on a group or individual basis takes place. It appears that safeguarding is a significant issue and there are existing procedures to follow. However, a timely reminder is often needed for the organisation to recognise this more often and not allow it to be underplayed and something which staff and volunteers must deal with on their own. There is a recognition that if voices were raised on an issue like this then management would be open to hearing about them, and action would then be required to lead on the issue:

---

[18] Participant B6.

[19] Participant B5.

Post pandemic we have more meetings and have more support given to one another. If I had a comment or suggestion which requires advocacy to make them happen, I do feel I would be listened to in a positive way. There feels a lot of openness and transparency, I guess.[20]

In situations taking place within the operation in Europe where asylum seekers have died or have disappeared or have gone missing, this is a difficult traumatic issue which for some staff is difficult to come to terms with:

The problem is that there's probably lots of people who have gone missing or have died and we have no idea. It upsets me. It would be nice to know what has happened to them or contact their friends and family as they will never know what's happened to them.[21]

It may be something which the organisation wishes to explore further. One potential approach would be to start a missing persons portal and database of those who have sadly gone missing. This would involve collecting information from asylum seekers and refugees which would need to be stored safely and in accordance with General Data Protection Regulations (GDPR).

As acknowledged earlier, capacity of staff is a challenge. There are not enough volunteers to support everybody and there is a limit which the organisation can do to meet the ever-growing need of asylum seekers and refugees. Consequently, volunteer retention is a significant issue. One of the reasons could be because of the financial barriers for volunteers which limit their involvement. It is found that there are monetary issues which affect some volunteers more than others:

We do not have a very diverse team of volunteers and that is down to the cost barriers that are in place for volunteering for us. People must pay for their transport to Europe, and they have to pay for their accommodation. Because of this we have a lot of volunteers who are from a middle-class background, and they tend to be white.[22]

---

[20] Participant B5.

[21] Participant B3.

[22] Participant B3.

Positively, they have many women volunteers. It has been stated that volunteers never work alone and therefore they do not have any safety concerns for their volunteers of any gender. As AX interact with many different types of races, nationalities and social groups who are asylum seekers, staff and volunteers are in a unique situation where they learn a lot about the experiences and journeys of those who are seeking to come to the UK. This is something which AX can celebrate but also has an emotional aspect to it too. A significant challenge is how could those asylum seekers and refugees AX help and support be incorporated into the organisation to support others because of their lived experience. Continuing to share the lived experience of asylum seekers and refugees through existing social media channels would be beneficial to those interested in being volunteers. Staff should be supported if they have a specific interest and skill in that area as one staff member outlines:

> I would welcome the opportunity to take on new things and try to help in other areas of the organisation. I'm interested in getting involved in external communications. I do a lot of this already by either speaking to the public or through social media and I would love to write posts and get involved in content creation as this is an effective way of sharing real life stories about asylum seekers and refugees.[23]

There is a need from some staff that the organisation would benefit from having a more diverse group of staff and volunteers. Having more ethnicities as part of the staff would be appreciated as diversity in any organisation is required. A challenge would be how does the organisation set out to address increasing the levels of diversity.

It is hoped that the above challenges are acknowledged by the senior management and leadership and for the Trustees of the organisation to look at the research and action potential improvements which will ultimately benefit the organisation, staff, volunteers and service users.

---

[23] Participant B2.

CHAPTER 9

# Conclusion

**Abstract** The conclusion summarises the main themes identified from the research. It explains the important work the organisation does and how it is a very much flexible and dynamic organisation, able to change speedily to a national and international event whilst not being compromised in their abilities to help and support asylum seekers. The research concludes on a very positive tone but acknowledges that there is more work to do to effectively assist asylum seekers and refugees now and moving forward into times which have been shown to be more politically hostile.

**Keywords** Asylum Seekers · Refugees · Politicalisation of Immigration

This research offered a fascinating insight into the issues and challenges an organisation were coping with during the pandemic whilst simultaneously assisting and supporting asylum seekers and refugees. It specifically explains how they overcome the problems which Covid-19 presented to the organisation and asylum seekers and refugees in seeking protection and support. The research presents an honest and accurate account of what happened during the pandemic and the impact it had on volunteers and staff within the charity, but also from the lived experience from asylum seekers and refugees. Therefore, the work offered a dual perspective to the issues involved.

The research positively detailed the challenges which were clearly identified by the charity and asylum seekers and explains how these were overcome so that asylum seekers and refugees were still able to successfully access the help and support from the organisation despite the social restrictions which were imposed by the Government at that time during the pandemic.

As we have seen, the research has highlighted what AX does for the benefit of asylum seekers and refugees both in the UK and in Europe, described some of the challenges they faced during the pandemic and afterwards along with examining the present issues associated with their work.

As it has been seen, once asylum seekers have had their asylum claims accepted by the Home Office and they have to leave temporary hotel accommodation, new challenges awaited them. Many have found it difficult to access suitable housing in time. Conclusively, on the one hand it is good news that claims are being processed which is a positive, but on the other hand, this is having a detrimental impact socially by a distinct lack of housing.

Without question, the organisation has commitment, passion and enthusiasm from people who work within the charity, it has lots of experience which then contribute to the huge effectiveness of the work done for asylum seekers. However, the impact of trauma on staff and volunteers cannot be overlooked or disregarded either.

Any small changes to how the organisation will adapt and change given the pandemic experience made will make a substantial and significant difference to the staff, volunteers, asylum seekers and refugees. Above all, the essential work undertaken and completed by staff and the relentless commitment from volunteers should never be overlooked nor is ever taken for granted. It is clear how asylum seekers and refugees immensely value the efforts and expertise they show to continue and increase the quality of advocacy for vulnerable individuals.

Their work continues to shine a bright light within the charitable sector, and it should never be able to be dimmed by the challenges asylum seekers and refugees face within the politically hostile rhetoric which surround the issue of migration and asylum. Despite the challenges and barriers which AX consistently and continuously overcome to make the lives of the people they serve more humane, they are unique in the contribution to the lives of marginalised individuals. Despite the issues, AX is well equipped to make any changes they see fit to move positively forward for the benefit of asylum seekers and refugees seeking a better life in the UK. This research clearly demonstrates this.

# Bibliography

## International Law

Article 25 of the Universal Declaration of Human Rights, United Nations
General Assembly in Paris on 10 December 1948—General Assembly resolution 217 A.

## Table of Statutes

Illegal Migration Act 2023.
Immigration and Asylum Act 1999.
Nationality & Borders Act 2022.
Safety of Rwanda (Asylum and Immigration) Bill, 7 March 2024, accessed at
https://bills.parliament.uk/publications/54559/documents/4541.

## Legislation Briefings

UK-Rwanda treaty: provision of an asylum partnership Published, 5 December
2023—https://www.gov.uk/government/publications/uk-rwanda-treaty-
provision-of-an-asylum-partnership/uk-rwanda-treaty-provision-of-an-asylum-
partnership-accessible.

## TABLE OF CASES

R (on the application of AAA (Syria) and others) (Respondents/Cross Appellants) v Secretary of State for the Home Department (Appellant/Cross Respondent) [2023] UKSC 42.

## JOURNALS

Denaro. C and Giuffre. M, 'UN Sustainable Development Goals and the "Refugee Gap": Leaving Refugees Behind?' (2022) Refugee Survey Quarterly, Vol 41, 79–107.

Hoare. T, Vidgen. A and Roberts. N.P, 'How do people seeking asylum in the United Kingdom conceptualize and cope with the asylum journey?' (2020) Medicine, Conflict and Survival 2020, Vol 36, No. 4, 333–358.

Liebling. H, Burke. S, Goodman. S and Zasada. D, 'Understanding the experiences of asylum seekers,' (2014) International Journal of Migration, Health, and Social Care, Vol 10 No. 4, 207.

Yeo. R, 'Disabled asylum seekers?...They don't really exist': The marginalisation of disabled asylum seekers in the UK and why it matters,' (2015) Disability and the Global South, Vol 2, No. 1, 523–550.

## HOUSE OF COMMONS BRIEFINGS

Georgina Sturge, 'Asylum statistics,' House of Commons Library, 1 March 2024.

Melanie Gower, 'Asylum accommodation: hotels, vessels and large-scale sites,' House of Commons Library, Research Briefing, 7 July 2023, accessed at https://researchbriefings.files.parliament.uk/documents/CBP-9831/CBP-9831.pdf.

Melanie Gower, 'Irregular migration: a timeline of UK-French cooperation,' Research briefing number 9681, House of Commons Library, 22 March 2023.

## UK GOVERNMENT STATISTICS

Home Office, Official Statistics Irregular migration to the UK, year ending June 2023, Updated 14 November 2023, accessed at https://www.gov.uk/government/statistics/irregular-migration-to-the-uk-year-ending-june-2023/irregular-migration-to-the-uk-year-ending-june-2023#:~:text=Of%20the%2010%2C377%20Albanian%20small,or%20another%20type%20of%20leave.

Home Office Data, 'Small boat activity in the English Channel,' 14th November 2024, accessed at https://www.gov.uk/government/publications/migrants-detected-crossing-the-english-channel-in-small-boats.

## Other Reports

Home Office, 'Ceasing Section 95 Support instruction,' Version 2.0, 7 July 2023, accessed at https://assets.publishing.service.gov.uk/media/64afb2fe8 bc29f000d2ccc78/Ceasing_Section_95_Support_Instruction.pdf.

Home Office Policy Paper, 'Memorandum of Understanding between the government of the United Kingdom of Great Britain and Northern Ireland and the government of the Republic of Rwanda for the provision of an asylum partnership arrangement,' 14 April 2022, accessed at https://www.gov.uk/government/publications/memorandum-of-understanding-mou-bet ween-the-uk-and-rwanda/memorandum-of-understanding-between-the-gov ernment-of-the-united-kingdom-of-great-britain-and-northern-ireland-and-the-government-of-the-republic-of-r.

Joe Tyler-Todd, Georgina Sturge and CJ McKinney, 'Delays to processing asylum claims in the UK,' Research Briefing Number CBP 9737, 20 March 2023.

Marine Accident Investigation Branch (MAIB) Accident Report, 'Report on the investigation into the flooding and partial sinking of an inflatable migrant boat resulting in the loss of at least 27 lives in the Dover Strait on 24 November 2021,' Report No 7/2023 November 2023.

Marley Morris and Amreen Qureshi, 'Understanding the Rise in Channel Crossings,' Institute for Public Policy Research, October 2022.

## Online Reports

Andy Hewett, 'Living in Limbo: A decade of delays in the UK asylum system,' July 2021 at 1, accessed at https://www.refugeecouncil.org.uk/wp-content/uploads/2021/07/Living-in-Limbo-A-decade-of-delays-in-the-UK-Asylum-system-July-2021.pdf.

British Medical Association, 'NHS backlog data analysis,' 15 March 2024, accessed at https://www.bma.org.uk/advice-and-support/nhs-delivery-and-workforce/pressures/nhs-backlog-data-analysis#:~:text=around%203.25%20m illion%20of%20these,December%202023%20figure%20of%20337%2C000.

International Organization for Migration (IOM), 'The Impacts of COVID-19 on Migration and Migrants from a Gender Perspective,' IOM, Geneva, 2022 at Xi, accessed at https://publications.iom.int/system/files/pdf/impacts-of-COVID-19-gender_1.pdf

Jack Larkham and Mariam Mansoor, 'Running hot, burning out,' Pro Bono Economics Nottingham Trent University, March 2023, accessed at https://www.probonoeconomics.com/Handlers/Download.ashx?IDMF=4690231e-ae66-4fbe-8a4e-9d51e16ed187.

Migration Observatory, 'People crossing the English Channel in small boats,' 21 July 2023, accessed at https://migrationobservatory.ox.ac.uk/resources/bri efings/people-crossing-the-english-channel-in-small-boats/.

Migration Observatory Research, 'The UK's asylum backlog,' 5 April 2023, accessed at https://migrationobservatory.ox.ac.uk/resources/briefings/the-uks-asylum-backlog/.

'Vicarious Trauma, Burnout and Staff Retention in the Anti-Slavery Sector,' Human Trafficking Foundation, August 2023, accessed at https://static1.squarespace.com/static/599abfb4e6f2e19ff048494f/t/64d3b77aad96c75 413e09c22/1691596666470/HTF+Post+Event+Briefing.pdf.

### NEWS REPORTS

BBC News, 'How many people cross the Channel in small boats and how many claim asylum in the UK,' accessed at https://www.bbc.co.uk/news/uk-536 99511.

Kate Whannel, 'UK to pay failed asylum seekers to move to Rwanda under new scheme,' *BBC News*, 13 March 2024, accessed at https://www.bbc.co.uk/news/uk-politics-68550404#:~:text=Failed%20asylum%20seekers%20are%20t o,return%20to%20their%20home%20country.

Home Office News, 'The use of temporary hotels to house asylum seekers during Covid-19,' 8 August 2020, accessed at https://homeofficemedia.blog.gov.uk/2020/08/08/the-use-of-temporary-hotels-to-house-asylum-see kers-during-covid-19/.

### NEWSPAPER REPORTS

Ben Morris, 'Record 5,000 cross Channel to UK in first three months of 2024,' *The Guardian*, 31 March 2024, accessed at https://www.theguardian.com/uk-news/2024/mar/31/record-number-channel-crossings-small-boats-uk-immigration.

Kwame Boakye, 'Refugees facing "life on the streets" without change to Home Office housing rules,' Local Government Chronicle, 15 January 2024.

Matthew Lodge and Greg Heffer, 'Asylum seekers are "gaming the system" to remain in the UK and "50% of migrants are adults pretending to be children", Suella Braverman claims just days after threatening to leave European Convention on Human Rights,' *The Guardian*, 29 September 2023, accessed at https://www.dailymail.co.uk/news/article-12576645/Asylum-seekers-gaming-remain-UK-50-migrants-adults-pretending-children-Suella-Braverman-claims-just-days-threatening-leave-European-Convention-Human-Rights.html.

Rajeev Syal, 'Home Office "loses" 17,000 people whose asylum claims were withdrawn,' *The Guardian*, 29 November 2023, accessed at https://www.theguardian.com/world/2023/nov/29/home-office-loses-17000-asylum-see kers-registered-in-britain.

## Government Press Releases

Prime Minister's Office Press Statement, 'Prime Minister agrees unprecedented measures to tackle illegal immigration alongside France,' 10 March 2023, accessed at https://www.gov.uk/government/news/prime-minister-agrees-unprecedented-measures-to-tackle-illegal-migration-alongside-france.

# Index

The manufacturer's authorised representative in the EU is Springer
Nature Customer Service Centre GmbH, Europaplatz 3, 69115 Heidelberg,
Germany. If you have any concerns regarding our products, please
contact ProductSafety@springernature.com

Printed and bound by CPI Group (UK) Ltd, Croydon, CR0 4YY

24/04/2026

02096370-0002